Alternative
Energy Sources

Other Books in the Current Controversies series

Current
CONTROVERSIES

Alternative Energy Sources

Darrin Gunkel, Book Editor

GREENHAVEN PRESS
A part of Gale, Cengage Learning

GALE
CENGAGE Learning

Detroit • New York • San Francisco • New Haven, Conn • Waterville, Maine • London

Bonnie Szumski, *Publisher*
Helen Cothran, *Managing Editor*

© 2006 Greenhaven Press, a part of Gale, Cengage Learning.

For more information, contact:
Greenhaven Press
27500 Drake Rd.
Farmington Hills, MI 48331-3535
Or you can visit our Internet site at gale.cengage.com

Articles in Greenhaven Press anthologies are often edited for length to meet page requirements. In addition, original titles of these works are changed to clearly present the main
thesis and to explicitly indicate the author's opinion. Every effort is made to ensure that
Greenhaven Press accurately reflects the original intent of the authors. Every effort has
been made to trace the owners of copyrighted material.

Cover photograph reproduced by permission of Lester Lefkowitz/CORBIS.

LIBRARY OF CONGRESS CATALOGING-IN-PUBLICATION DATA

Library of Congress Control Number: 2006929510

Printed in the United States of America
3 4 5 6 7   13 12 11 10 09

ED105

Contents

Chapter 4: Should Alternative Fuels Be Pursued?

Foreword

By definition, controversies are "discussions of questions in which opposing opinions clash" (*Webster's Twentieth Century Dictionary Unabridged*). Few would deny that controversies are a pervasive part of the human condition and exist on virtually every level of human enterprise. Controversies transpire between individuals and among groups, within nations and between nations. Controversies supply the grist necessary for progress by providing challenges and challengers to the status quo. They also create atmospheres where strife and warfare can flourish. A world without controversies would be a peaceful world; but it also would be, by and large, static and prosaic.

The Series' Purpose

The purpose of the Current Controversies series is to explore many of the social, political, and economic controversies dominating the national and international scenes today. Titles selected for inclusion in the series are highly focused and specific. For example, from the larger category of criminal justice, Current Controversies deals with specific topics such as police brutality, gun control, white collar crime, and others. The debates in Current Controversies also are presented in a useful, timeless fashion. Articles and book excerpts included in each title are selected if they contribute valuable, long-range ideas to the overall debate. And wherever possible, current information is enhanced with historical documents and other relevant materials. Thus, while individual titles are current in focus, every effort is made to ensure that they will not become quickly outdated. Books in the Current Controversies series will remain important resources for librarians, teachers, and students for many years.

In addition to keeping the titles focused and specific, great care is taken in the editorial format of each book in the series. Book introductions and chapter prefaces are offered to provide background material for readers. Chapters are organized around several key questions that are answered with diverse opinions representing all points on the political spectrum. Materials in each chapter include opinions in which authors clearly disagree as well as alternative opinions in which authors may agree on a broader issue but disagree on the possible solutions. In this way, the content of each volume in Current Controversies mirrors the mosaic of opinions encountered in society. Readers will quickly realize that there are many viable answers to these complex issues. By questioning each author's conclusions, students and casual readers can begin to develop the critical thinking skills so important to evaluating opinionated material.

Current Controversies is also ideal for controlled research. Each anthology in the series is composed of primary sources taken from a wide gamut of informational categories including periodicals, newspapers, books, United States and foreign government documents, and the publications of private and public organizations. Readers will find factual support for reports, debates, and research papers covering all areas of important issues. In addition, an annotated table of contents, an index, a book and periodical bibliography, and a list of organizations to contact are included in each book to expedite further research.

Perhaps more than ever before in history, people are confronted with diverse and contradictory information. During the Persian Gulf War, for example, the public was not only treated to minute-to-minute coverage of the war, it was also inundated with critiques of the coverage and countless analyses of the factors motivating U.S. involvement. Being able to sort through the plethora of opinions accompanying today's major issues, and to draw one's own conclusions, can be a complicated and frustrating struggle. It is the editors' hope that Current Controversies will help readers with this struggle.

Introduction

"As world energy usage increases and energy supplies decrease, the controversy over energy independence will only intensify."

When people hear the words "alternative energy," one of the first things that jumps to mind is the environment. They conjure up images of clean, white windmills replacing smoke-belching power plants, and they envision sleek hydrogen cars that emit nothing more than water. Environmental considerations are certainly central to debates about energy alternatives, but perhaps even more important in some analysts' view is the economic impact. The U.S. economy depends completely on ample supplies of inexpensive energy. In consequence, any decisions made concerning energy necessarily affect the economy as well.

One of the economic concerns in the energy debate is energy independence. Many experts worry that the United States is too dependent on foreign sources of oil, claiming that such dependence makes the country vulnerable to supply disruptions. Some of these analysts recommend a transition to renewable energy sources in order to wean the nation off of foreign oil. Others advocate for increased domestic oil and gas drilling. Still other commentators disagree with both of these proposals, contending that energy independence is not a worthwhile goal. In their minds, transitioning from cheap foreign oil will negatively impact the economy. As world energy usage increases and energy supplies decrease, the controversy over energy independence will only intensify.

America's reliance on foreign oil has been an increasing concern among policy makers. According to the U.S. Department of Energy, America imports 56 percent of the oil it uses, and that figure is predicted to rise to 68 percent by the year 2025. Transportation—not just the cars and planes that individuals use to get around, but the trucks and trains that move goods from farms and factories to markets—is such a vital part of the American economy that many experts are beginning to question the wisdom of relying so heavily on imported oil to keep it running. As Illinois senator Barack Obama puts it, "For all of our military might and economic dominance, the Achilles heel of the most powerful country on earth is the oil we cannot live without." The cost of imported oil now accounts for about one-third of the U.S. trade deficit, the amount by which imports to the United States exceed exports. If that gap becomes too great, many commentators claim, America's economic stability may be threatened. Some economists fear that the gap will continue to grow, in part because of increased fuel demand.

To address the problem, many experts advocate for a transition to renewable energy sources such as solar and wind power. The federal government has also endorsed such a shift, encouraging the development of alternatives by offering subsidies. Subsidies, the government believes, can help renewables compete with fossil fuels while scientists continue to make renewable energy sources more competitive. Not everyone agrees that subsidies are a good idea, however. A report by the Competitive Enterprise Institute in Washington, D.C., questions the effects such subsidies have on America's free market system. "While these programs may be relatively small given the size of domestic energy markets," the institute asserts, "they serve little, if any, useful purpose while subsidizing large corporations at taxpayer expense."

Investing in energy alternatives is just one idea of how to increase America's energy independence. Other experts say that America should increase domestic oil and gas drilling. Much of this drilling would require opening up public lands to energy development. One area under scrutiny is the Arctic

National Wildlife Refuge (ANWR), which many scientists believe contains at least a ten-year supply of oil. Drilling advocates consider the environmental costs of drilling in ANWR small compared to the economic benefits. Domestic drilling, however, is hugely controversial. Environmentalists claim that drilling in ANWR, for example, would destroy a pristine wilderness, harming the caribou and other wildlife that live there.

Still other experts stress how domestic energy development can help the economy by creating jobs. It takes workers to build and operate energy refineries and power plants, and to make sure energy is somehow transported to consumers who buy it. Promoting job growth in the United States is a topic of increasing interest as more and more traditional American jobs are outsourced to other countries. Alternative energy development can help fill that gap, according to a report released in 2004 by scientists at the University of California–Berkeley. The researchers estimate that if 20 percent of the country's energy were to come from renewable sources, then between 188,018 and 240,850 new jobs could be created by the year 2020. While many of those concerned about job creation think development of renewables is the best solution, other observers point out that *any* domestic energy production, including oil and gas drilling, can create jobs.

While many experts wrangle over how to achieve energy independence, others contend that the debate is hardly relevant. To their way of thinking, the key to the health of the U.S. economy is to make sure it grows rapidly enough so that the trade deficit remains relatively small compared to the overall size of the economy. One way to ensure such growth, they argue, is to guarantee that the United States has a steady supply of inexpensive energy regardless of where it comes from. In this scenario, alternative energy sources and domestic oil are both a problem, simply because they cannot compete economically with foreign oil. Justin Fox, editor-at-large for *Fortune* magazine, argues, "The simplest way to get the most out of what we spend on energy is to keep energy costs cheap, and the best way to do that is to take full advantage of global energy markets."

The debate over energy independence illustrates how complex energy policies are. Any energy decision will have a multitude of environmental and economic impacts that will continue to affect the country well into the future. Many of these costs are explored in *Current Controversies: Alternative Energy Sources*. In this anthology, authors examine whether alternative energy sources can help end foreign oil dependence and whether energy independence is a goal worth pursuing.

Should Alternative Energy Replace Conventional Energy?

Chapter Preface

When the new "Building 7" of the World Trade Center opened in New York City in March 2006, it marked the first step in rebuilding the center after the September 11, 2001, terrorist attacks leveled it. The structure also became the city's first certified "green" building, incorporating new environmentally friendly designs. One of the hallmarks of green buildings, according to the U.S. Green Building Council, is their use of energy-efficiency technology. In exploring the question of whether or not alternative energy sources should replace conventional energy, many experts are now stressing that such a transition would not be required if Americans learned to conserve the energy they have. Or, to look at it another way, if Americans could capture the energy lost in production and consumption—which some refer to as alternative energy—they would not need to explore new energy sources.

Indeed, many energy experts consider energy efficiency a kind of vast alternative energy supply, waiting to be tapped. Some power plants, for example, are beginning to recapture energy that would otherwise be wasted in the form of escaped heat, and selling it. Energy efficiency not only reduces fuel costs but can increase profits as well. Furthermore, advocates argue that efficiency is the best way to meet growing demand, eliminating the need to build new power plants or to drill or mine for new fossil fuels. According to researchers at the Rocky Mountain Institute in Snowmass, Colorado, the technology exists today to cut energy consumption by 75 percent or more. A report from the U.S. Department of Energy asserts that mandating energy-efficient appliances will save American consumers $150 billion by the year 2050.

But many researchers disagree. The Cato Institute in Washington, D.C., argues that federal rules mandating energy-efficient appliances will actually cost American consumers $50 billion by the year 2050. The institute claims that consumers will pay more for energy-efficient appliances than they will recoup from the energy they save. Furthermore, critics of energy conservation argue, adopting energy efficiency as a strategy will require significant lifestyle changes that many Americans will not be willing to make. They question whether Americans are really willing to drive less or turn down air conditioners in hot weather. Moreover, raising automobile fuel-efficiency standards would necessitate smaller vehicles that would be more dangerous for the cars' occupants, these critics maintain.

Pursuing any form of alternative energy will likely mean big changes in infrastructure, habits, and the economy. In the following chapter the authors debate whether a transition to alternatives is necessary. The debate over energy efficiency illustrates how difficult it can be to create a viable energy policy.

The World Is Running Out of Oil

Tony Black

Tony Black is a contributing writer to Canadian Dimension, *a magazine advancing progressive viewpoints.*

According ... to many of the world's most prestigious (independent) oil geologists and institutions, not only is the era of cheap oil now almost certainly at an end, but by the end of this decade [2000–09]—and likely before—the price of a barrel of oil will rise well past $100, and will continue to climb quickly and inexorably thereafter. One need not be a rocket scientist to begin to grasp the staggering implications of this for industrial civilization.

But before we do that, best to start at the beginning. . . .

The Problem

In 1956, the geologist M. King Hubbert predicted that the U.S.'s oil production would peak in 1970, and thereafter begin an accelerating decline. Despite being derided at the time by many industry analysts, his predictions proved entirely accurate. This, for the very good reason that he had correctly figured out that oil extraction follows a statistical model known as a bell curve.

Oil production starts off slow, picks up more and more, reaches a peak—when half the oil has been pumped out—and then begins to fall as it had risen, that is, faster and faster. In the latter stages, all sorts of strategies are used to maintain pressure at the well-head, including pumping the reservoir with water and gas. Still, it's a case finally of diminishing returns. Less and less oil at greater and greater cost.

Tony Black, "The Party's (Almost) Over," *Canadian Dimension*, vol. 39, September-October 2005, p. 14. Reproduced by permission of the author.

But, you might ask, what difference does it make if a particular oil field runs dry? Aren't new ones being discovered?

Even the largest oil field in the world, the giant Ghawar of Saudi Arabia, is showing distinct signs of having peaked.

In fact, many of the world's largest oil fields are now decades old and are depleting rapidly. Thus, in the mid-eighties the North Sea used to produce 500,000 barrels per day. Today it produces 50,000. Prudhoe Bay in Alaska once gushed out over 1.5 million barrels per day, but in 1989 it peaked and now gives only 350,000. The huge Russian Samotlor field used to account for 3.5 million barrels per day. Now its ledger tallies a mere 350,000.

Even the largest oil field in the world, the giant Ghawar of Saudi Arabia, is showing distinct signs of having peaked. The Saudis must now inject some seven million barrels of water per day into the reservoir just to maintain well-head pressure.

As for new discoveries, there have been no new large discoveries in over two decades. The 14 largest oil fields average over forty years old. Indeed, Dr. Colin Campbell, former chief geologist for Shell Oil, has stated that the discovery of major new oil reserves "peaked in the 1960s" and that, "We now find one barrel for every four we consume."

'Peak oil' will likely be upon us sometime before 2010.

"Peak Oil Is Near"

According to the best estimates, by such as the Petro-consultants of Geneva, the French Petroleum Institute and the Colorado School of Mines, global "peak oil" will likely be upon us sometime before 2010. Such estimates, of course, fly in the face of those by the U.S. Geological Survey and the International Energy Agency, both of which acknowledge "peak oil," but which project its onset to somewhere between 2015 and 2040. Most of the independent experts, however, argue that these latter figures are mistaken on at least three counts.

The first is that oil reserve figures have been inflated for years for purely speculative and ideological reasons, essentially to maintain investor confidence. A stark illustration is provided by the scandal of Shell Oil, which was recently forced to revise its reserve estimates downwards by over twenty per cent.

The second involves reliance on so-called "non-conventional" oil supplies, including tar sands and oil shales. Unfortunately, these require massive amounts of energy to extract. And not just energy. For every barrel of oil from tar sands, 400 to 1,000 cubic feet of gas are required. For every barrel of oil from shale, one to four barrels of water are needed. Moreover, the trailings and detritus left behind are literally mountainous, an environmental nightmare just waiting to explode.

The gap between [oil] demand and supply is already beginning to yawn.

They also take time to bring on line. It is expected, for instance, that Canada will, by 2030, be producing no more than four million barrels of oil per day from its Athabascan oil sands. This would amount to little more than three per cent of the (now widely agreed upon) estimated global need of 120 million barrels per day (mb/d) by 2025 to 2030. (Present usage is about 84 mb/d.)

Finally, the term "peak oil" refers not just to the problem of declining rates of discovery and extraction, but also to the compounding problem of increasing rates of consumption. China, for instance, has recently surpassed Japan as the world's second-largest importer of oil, imports which are rising by nine per cent a year. India's thirst is also exploding.

In short, the gap between demand and supply is already beginning to yawn. Once the downhill side of the bell curve sets in, this gap is likely to spread into a chasm. And the consequences of that are little short of catastrophic.

Good-bye Growth, Good-bye Globalization

For the past century, the world's industrial societies have enjoyed between two and seven per cent annual economic growth. This growth has been almost entirely fuelled by a bonanza of cheap, easily extractable, high grade oil. Virtually every aspect of our modern industrial economy relies on it, including global transport of goods, commercial air travel, gasoline for cars, the lubrication of industrial machinery, the generation of electricity and the production of plastics, fertilizers and pesticides. The consequences of, say, $150 per barrel of oil will profoundly affect everything from our suburban, commuting way of life right through to our industrial and international modes of agricultural production and distribution.

And that's just to begin with. World economic growth will likely become a quaint curiosity consigned to the history books. Permanent recession, if not outright depression, could well become the norm. Unemployment will undoubtedly skyrocket, as will world political instability. Driving a car? Taking a plane? These will gradually, incrementally, become elitist activities reserved for the few. Agriculture will need to become regionalized and localized, just as our whole modern way of life will need to be re-engineered to accommodate our changed energy circumstances.

Given all this, one might be hard pressed to comprehend how officialdom and the major media have failed both to recognize and/or respond adequately to the problem.

The narrow answer to this conundrum is that official reports have, for years, simply concentrated on global oil reserves (which are still quite extensive), rather than on the projected future gap between production and consumption. Thus, the world will continue to "enjoy" significant reserves far into the future. Oil will not, all of a sudden, simply run out. But the gap between supply and demand will grow quickly. Price volatility will follow suit.

The broad answer is, of course, that certain government bodies have already responded to the problem.

Resource Wars of the 21st Century

That the [2003 United States] invasion of Iraq was mostly about oil will come as no earth-shattering revelation to many. What is perhaps less well appreciated is how completely the list of nations comprising [President George W.] Bush & Co.'s "axis of evil" [Iraq, Iran, and North Korea] extend along an arc that maps virtually one-to-one both to the world's major reserves of oil, and to the strategic chokepoints and sea lanes vital to its transport and distribution.

The struggle, the war if you like, for the globe's limited energy resources has . . . already begun.

U.S. threats against Iran, for example, not only target one of the world's largest reserves of oil and the critical Strait of Hormuz, linking the Persian Gulf to the Arabian Sea, but also China itself, which has signed major oil deals with Iran. China's energy supplies and supply lines are further threatened by the U.S.'s sudden humanitarian interest in the Darfur region of the Sudan, where China also has major oil concessions; and by U.S. actions against Venezuela, with whom China has recently negotiated a major bilateral energy deal; and by Washington's recent naval and troop deployments to the Strait of Malacca, which controls access to the South China Sea. . . .

Analogous considerations apply to a host of other countries from Yemen and Somalia (straddling the vital oil-transit strait to the Red Sea) to Algeria (90 per cent of whose oil goes to Europe) to a string of countries girding the belly of Russia.

With respect to the latter, a very interesting contest is shaping up in the Caspian Sea basin. The American-backed Baku-Ceyhan pipeline (bringing oil westward and bypassing Russian pipelines) has recently been completed and the Kazakhstan-China oil pipeline is expected to come on line near the end of the decade. Meanwhile, though China and India have squared off in Angola, Indonesia and the Sudan, they have also engaged in intensive negotiations with respect to their energy security needs in Central Asia. There is talk of extending the Iran-Pakistan-India gas pipeline to eastern China.

The recent spate of "velvet" revolutions in Central Asia are clearly tied in with the American attempt to control this vital, energy-rich region. Overall, Russia, China and India are, in a very real sense, strategic allies who share common cause both in frustrating Washington's attempt to isolate Iran, and in securing sources and transit routes from the oil-rich Middle East and Central Asia to oil-deficient East Asia.

In summary, the struggle, the war if you like, for the globe's limited energy resources has, in other words, already begun.

To transition to the post-oil era . . . many experts have said would take a minimum twenty-year effort.

Sleepwalking into the Future

Are alternative fuels and alternative technologies the answers to the coming crisis?

The short reply is, possibly yes, probably no. Gas, for instance, is being touted as a clean alternative fuel. Unfortunately, gas is not only running out fast, but its depletion curve has the peculiar property that, when it does run out, it stops suddenly, with little warning. Moreover, to tap, say, Russia's great reserves of methane, it has first to be liquefied, at great cost, for transportation.

But then what about the renewables? Well, bio-fuel requires fertilizers—which require oil. In any case, land is needed, it's hardly necessary to add, to grow food. Hydrogen is clean, but it takes a lot of energy to produce it. A hydrogen economy is, really, no more than a fantasy. Wind and solar power are unlikely to ever significantly substitute for fossil fuels, at least given our present energy-intensive lifestyles. Nuclear is also being touted once again, but its capital and decommissioning costs are exorbitant and its nuclear waste problematic. Moreover, uranium is also a limited resource.

This leaves only a multi-faceted approach in which our remaining reserves of oil and gas are used to transition to a combination wind, solar and coal energy economy, while we simultaneously embark on mass-scale efficiencies, conservation and downscaling of our energy usage. It will be a different world. This in the best of scenarios, where immediate action is taken to transition to the post-oil era, a period many experts have said would take a minimum twenty-year effort.

But given how little open recognition there is of the problem, let alone any concerted worldwide policy to implement change, it seems rather more likely that, intoxicated for an entire century with the heady brew of cheap energy, the party will continue to rage on. That is, until the fridge runs dry, the tempers wear thin and the furniture is tipped, unceremoniously, on end.

Fossil Fuel Use Causes Global Warming

Mark Lynas

Mark Lynas is a journalist and environmental activist.

Hardly anyone realises it, but the debate about climate change is over. Scientists around the world have now amassed an unassailable body of evidence to support the conclusion that a warming of our planet—caused principally by greenhouse gas emissions from burning fossil fuel—is under way.

The dwindling band of climate "sceptics", a rag-tag bunch of oil and coal industry frontmen, retired professors and semi-deranged obsessives, is now on the defensive. . . .

Global Changes

Meanwhile the world as we once knew it is beginning to unravel. The signs are everywhere, even in Britain. Horse chestnut, oak and ash trees are coming into leaf more than a week earlier than two decades ago. The growing season now lasts almost all year round: in 2000 there were just 39 official days of winter.

Destructive winter floods are part of this warming trend, while in lowland England snow has become a thing of the past. Where I live in Oxford, six out of the past ten winters have been completely snowless—something that happened only twice during the whole 30-year period between 1960 and 1990. The rate of warming has now become so rapid that it is equivalent to your garden moving south by 20 metres every single day.

In other parts of the world, the signs of global warming are more dramatic. [From 2000 to 2003], researching a book

Mark Lynas, "It's Later Than You Think." *New Statesman*, vol. 16, June 30, 2003, p. 16. Copyright © 2003 New Statesman, Ltd. Reproduced by permission.

on the subject, I have witnessed major climate-driven changes across five continents, changes that are leaving millions homeless, destitute and in danger.

Alaska Is Warming

In Alaska I spent a week in the Eskimo village of Shishmaref, on the state's remote western coast, just 70 miles from the eastern coast of Russia. While the midnight sun shone outside, I listened as the village elder, Clifford Weyiouanna, told me how the sea, which used to freeze in October, was now ice-free until Christmas. And even when the sea ice does eventually form, he explained, it is so thin that it is dangerous to walk and hunt on. The changing seasons are also affecting the animals: seals and walruses—still crucial elements of the Eskimo diet—are migrating earlier and are almost impossible to catch. The whole village caught only one walrus [in 2002], after covering thousands of miles by boat.

Shishmaref lives in perpetual fear. The cliffs on which the 600-strong community sits are thawing, and during the last big storm 50 feet of ground was lost overnight. People battled 90mph winds to save their houses from the crashing waves.

In Fairbanks, Alaska ... bears had become so confused [by the warmer weather] they didn't know whether to hibernate or stay awake.

I stood on the shoreline [in 2002] with Robert Iyatunguk, the co-ordinator of the Shishmaref Erosion Coalition, looking up at a house left hanging over the clifftop. "The wind is getting stronger, the water is getting higher, and it's noticeable to everybody in town," he told me. "It just kind of scares you inside your body and makes you wonder exactly when the big one is going to hit." In July 2002 the residents voted to abandon the site altogether—a narrow barrier island that has been continuously occupied by Eskimos for centuries—and move elsewhere.

In Fairbanks, Alaska's main town in the interior, everyone talks about warming. The manager of the hostel where I stayed, a keen hunter, told me how ducks had been swimming on the river in December (it's supposed to freeze over in autumn), how bears had become so confused they didn't know whether to hibernate or stay awake, and that winter temperatures, which used to plummet to 40 degrees below zero, now barely touched 25 below.

All around the town, roads are buckling and houses sagging as the permafrost underneath them thaws. In one house, the occupants, a cleaning lady and her daughter, showed me that to walk across the kitchen meant going uphill (the house was tilting sideways) and how shelves had to be rebalanced with bits of wood to stop everything falling off. Other dwellings have been abandoned. New ones are built on adjustable stilts.

The Impact in China

Scientists have long predicted that global warming will lead in some places to intense flooding and drought. When I visited China in April [2002], the country's northern provinces were in the grip of the worst drought in more than a century. Entire lakes had dried up, and in many places sand dunes were advancing across the farmers' fields.

One lakeside village in Gansu Province, just off the old Silk Road, was abandoned after the waters dried up—apart from one woman, who lives amid the ruins with a few chickens and a cow for company. "Of course I'm lonely!" she cried in answer to my rather insensitive question. "Can you imagine how boring this life is? I can't move; I can do nothing. I have no relatives, no friends and no money." She was tormented by memories of how it had once been, when neighbours had chatted and swapped stories late into the evenings, before the place became a ghost town.

Minutes after I had left, a dust storm blew in. These storms are getting more frequent, and even Beijing is now hit repeatedly every spring. During an earlier visit to a remote village in eastern Inner Mongolia, not far from the ruins of Kubla Khan's fabled Xanadu, I experienced an even stronger storm. Day was turned into night as a blizzard of sand and dust scoured the mud-brick buildings. I cowered inside one house with a Mongolian peasant family, sharing rice wine and listening to tales of how the grass had once grown waist-high on the surrounding plains. Now the land is little more than arid desert, thanks to persistent drought and overgrazing. The storm raged for hours. When it eased in the late afternoon and the sun appeared again, the village cockerels crowed, thinking that morning had come early.

Hundreds of millions of people will suffer water shortages as their source glaciers decline over the coming century.

Mountain Glaciers Are Shrinking

The drought in north-west China is partly caused by shrinking run-off from nearby mountains, which because of the rising temperatures are now capped with less snow and ice than before. Glacier shrinkage is a phenomenon repeated across the world's mountain ranges, and I also saw it at first hand in Peru, standing dizzy with altitude sickness in the high Andes 5,200 metres above the capital, Lima, where one of the main water-supplying glaciers has shrunk by more than a kilometre during the past century.

A senior manager of Lima's water authority told me later how melting ice is now a critical threat to future freshwater supplies: this city of seven million is the world's second-largest desert metropolis after Cairo, and the mountains supply all its water through coastal rivers that pour down from the ice fields far above. It is the snows that keep the rivers running all year round—once the glaciers are gone, the rivers will flow only in the wet season. The same problem afflicts the Indian subcontinent: overwhelmingly dependent on the mighty Ganges, Indus and Brahmaputra rivers that flow from the Himalayas, hundreds of millions of people will suffer water shortages as their source glaciers decline over the coming century.

A warming during this century alone of up to six degrees Celsius . . . would take the earth into dangerous uncharted waters.

Islands Are Flooding

Unless alternative water supplies can be secured, Lima will be left depopulated, its people scattered as environmental refugees. This is a category already familiar to the residents of Tuvalu, a group of nine coral atolls in the middle of the Pacific. Tuvalu, together with Kiribati, the Maldives and many other island nations, has made its plight well known to the world community, and an evacuation plan—shifting 75 people each year to New Zealand—is already under way.

I saw at first hand how the islands are already affected by the rising sea level, paddling in knee-deep floodwaters during [2002's] spring tides, which submerged much of Funafuti and almost surrounded the airstrip. Later that same evening the country's first post-independence prime minister, Toaripi Lauti, told me of his shock at finding his own crop of pulaka (a root vegetable like taro, grown in sunken pits) dying from saltwater intrusion. He recalled how everyone had awoken one morning a few years previously to find that one of the islets on the atoll's rim had disappeared from the horizon, washed over by the waves, its coconut trees smashed and destroyed by the rising sea.

However severe these unfolding climate-change impacts seem, they are—like the canary in the coal mine—just the first whispers of the holocaust that lies ahead if nothing is done to reduce greenhouse gas emissions. Scientists meeting under the banner of the UN-sponsored Intergovernmental Panel on Climate Change (IPCC) have predicted a warming during this century alone of up to six degrees Celsius, which would take the earth into dangerous uncharted waters. . . . Scientists at the UK's Hadley Centre reported that the warming might be even greater because of the complexities of the carbon cycle.

The IPCC's worst-case forecast of six degrees could prove almost unimaginably catastrophic. It took only six degrees of warming to spark the end-Permian mass extinction 251 million years ago, the worst crisis ever to hit life on earth (expertly chronicled by Michael Benton in *When Life Nearly Died*), which led to the deaths of 95 per cent of all species alive at the time.

Current reserves alone include enough oil, coal and gas utterly to destabilise the world's climate. Searching for more is [illogical and wasteful].

If humanity is to avoid a similar fate, global greenhouse gas emissions need to be brought down to between 60 and 80 percent below current levels—precisely the reverse of emissions forecasts recently produced by the International Energy Agency. A good start would be the ratification and speedy implementation of the Kyoto Protocol, [an international treaty to reduce fossil fuel emissions,] which should be superseded after the following decade by the "contraction and convergence" model proposed by the Global Commons Institute in London (www.gci.org.uk), allocating equal per-person emissions rights among all the world's nations.

"No New Oil"

In the meantime, a network of campaigning groups is currently mobilising under the banner of "No new oil", demanding an end to the exploration and development of new fossil fuel reserves, on the basis that current reserves alone include enough oil, coal and gas utterly to destabilise the world's climate. Searching for more is just as illogical as it is wasteful.

Avoiding dangerous climate change and other large-scale environmental crises will need to become the key organising principle around which societies evolve. All the signs are that few in power realise this—least of all the current US administration [of George W. Bush], which has committed itself to a policy of wanton destructiveness, with control and exploitation of oil supplies a central theme.

We must abandon the old mindset that demands an oil-based economy, not just because it sparks wars and terrorism, but because the future of life on earth depends on leaving it behind.

Coal-Fired Power Plants Produce Dangerous Mercury Emissions

Emily Figdor

Emily Figdor is a campaigner with the U.S. Public Interest Research Group, a nonprofit consumer and environmental advocacy organization.

Editor's note: In March 2005, seven months after the release of the report from which this viewpoint is taken, President George W. Bush signed a law requiring coal power plants to reduce mercury emissions. Many environmental groups claim, however, that the law does not reduce those emissions enough to protect public health.

M ercury emissions from coal-fired power plants and other industrial sources are making the fish in our lakes, rivers, and streams unsafe to eat. Coal-fired power plants are by far the nation's largest unregulated source of mercury emissions, contributing 41 percent of all U.S. mercury emissions. The mercury deposits in soil and surface waters, where bacteria convert it to a highly toxic form of mercury that bioaccumulates in fish, including popular sport and commercial fish. This report analyzes new data from the U.S. Environmental Protection Agency (EPA) to determine the extent to which fish in the nation's lakes are contaminated with mercury. . . .

Key findings include the following:

- All of the fish samples were contaminated with mercury.

- Fifty-five (55) percent of the fish samples were contaminated with mercury at levels that exceed EPA's
  "safe" limit for women of average weight who eat fish
  twice a week. In 29 states, mercury levels in at least half
  of the fish samples exceeded this limit.

- Seventy-six (76) percent of the fish samples exceeded
  the safe mercury limit for children of average weight
  under age three who eat fish twice a week; 63 percent
  of fish samples exceeded the limit for children ages
  three to five years; and 47 percent of the fish samples
  exceeded the limit for children six to eight years.

- Predator fish, or fish at the top of the aquatic food
  chain, had the highest average levels of mercury. Small-
  mouth bass, walleye, largemouth bass, lake trout, and
  Northern pike had the highest average mercury concentrations.

- Eighty (80) percent of the predator fish samples contained mercury levels exceeding EPA's safe limit for
  women. In 18 states, 100 percent of the predator fish
  samples exceeded this limit.

---

*Industrial sources [other than power plants] have re-
duced their mercury emissions by more than 90 percent
within a few short years.*

Mercury pollution is pervasive in the nation's lakes. Every
fish sample EPA tested was contaminated with mercury, and
the majority of the fish samples were contaminated with mercury at levels that could pose a public health risk. The results
underscore the need to reduce mercury emissions to the great-
est extent possible, as fast as possible.

Other industrial sources have reduced their mercury emissions by more than 90 percent within a few short years, but

power plants continue to emit unlimited amounts of mercury into the air. . . .

Health Effects of Mercury

Methylmercury, an organic form of mercury that accumulates in fish, is a potent neurotoxin. Eating contaminated fish is the primary way people are exposed to methylmercury in the U.S.

When pregnant women eat mercury-contaminated fish, methylmercury crosses the placenta to the fetus. It then accumulates in the brain, where it interferes with the growth and migration of neurons and can cause irreversible damage to the developing central nervous system. Extremely high doses of methylmercury, such as those that occurred in Minamata, Japan, starting in the 1950s and [in] Iraq in the early 1970s, can result in death and severe disabilities, including mental retardation, seizure disorders, cerebral palsy, blindness, and deafness, among children exposed in utero. At much lower doses, children exposed to methylmercury in utero can exhibit deficits in several brain functions, including attention, language, verbal memory, spatial function, and motor speed (reaction time). These more subtle impairments are still evident at ages seven and 14 years, suggesting that the effect of mercury on the developing brain is irreversible.

Mercury can affect multiple organ systems, including the nervous system, heart, and immune system, throughout an individual's lifespan.

In a 2000 review of the health effects of mercury, the National Academy of Sciences Committee on the Toxicological Effects of Methylmercury found the evidence of the neurodevelopmental effects of methylmercury "extensive." The panel stated, "Chronic, low-dose prenatal [methylmercury] exposure from maternal consumption of fish has been associated with more subtle end points of neurotoxicity in children. Those end points include poor performance on neurobehavioral tests, particularly on tests of attention, fine-motor function, language, visual-spatial abilities (e.g., drawing), and verbal memory." The panel concluded, "The population at highest risk is the children of women who consumed large amounts of fish and seafood during pregnancy. The committee concludes that the risk to that population is likely to be sufficient to result in an increase in the number of children who have to struggle to keep up in school and who might require remedial classes or special education."

In early 2004, EPA scientists estimated that one in six women of childbearing age in the U.S. has levels of methylmercury in her blood that are sufficiently high to put 630,000 of the four million babies born each year at risk of learning disabilities, developmental delays, and problems with fine motor coordination, among other problems. This figure is a doubling of previous estimates based on increasing evidence that methylmercury concentrates in the umbilical cord, exposing the developing fetus to higher levels of mercury than previously understood. Leading researchers in the field suggest that the figure is still an underestimate.

Coal-fired power plants are by far the largest unregulated source of mercury emissions in the U.S.

While the developing brain is thought to be most sensitive to the effects of methylmercury, mercury can affect multiple organ systems, including the nervous system, heart, and immune system, throughout an individual's lifespan. Adults exposed to methylmercury from fish may experience neurocognitive deficits similar to those seen in children exposed prenatally. In addition, higher mercury levels have been associated with an increased risk of heart attacks, leading researchers to conclude that "[h]igh mercury content may diminish the cardioprotective effect of fish intake." These results point to the need to be concerned about the consumption of mercury-contaminated fish among people of all ages and gender.

The Sources of Mercury

Since mercury is an element, it cannot be created or destroyed. The same amount has existed on the planet since the earth was formed. Natural processes, such as weathering of rock containing mercury, and human activities, such as combustion of coal containing mercury, mobilize and release mercury and cause it to cycle in the environment.

Coal-fired power plants are by far the largest unregulated source of mercury emissions in the U.S. In 1999, they emitted 48 tons of mercury, or 41 percent of U.S. mercury emissions. . . . The next largest source category is emissions from industrial and commercial boilers at 10 tons per year, or eight percent of emissions.

Unlike all other major sources of mercury emissions, power plants can emit unlimited amounts of mercury into the air. A decade ago, medical and municipal waste incinerators rivaled power plants in their mercury emissions. However, in the mid-1990s, EPA passed rules to reduce mercury emissions from these sources by 90 percent.

In 1990, medical waste incinerators emitted 50 tons of mercury, or 26 percent of U.S. mercury emissions. By 1999, they generated 2.8 tons, or 2 percent of U.S. mercury emissions. In 1990, municipal waste incinerators emitted 42 tons of mercury, or 22 percent of U.S. mercury emissions. By 1999, they released 5.1 tons, or 4 percent of U.S. mercury emissions.

In contrast, power plant emissions of mercury have remained largely unchanged, and their contribution to total U.S. mercury emissions has increased from 26 to more than 40 percent over the past decade. In addition, power plant mer-

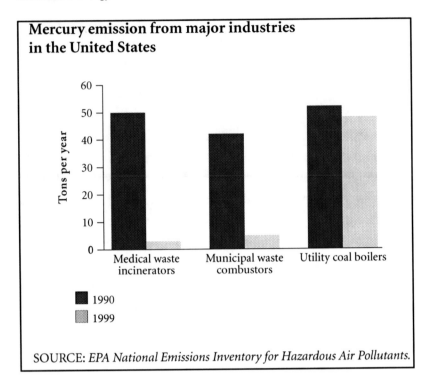

Mercury emission from major industries in the United States

Tons per year

1990
1999

Medical waste incinerators
Municipal waste combustors
Utility coal boilers

SOURCE: *EPA National Emissions Inventory for Hazardous Air Pollutants.*

cury emissions are expected to increase in the coming years due to a projected 26 percent increase in coal consumption by 2020. . . .

Mercury Deposition

EPA has concluded that "[m]ost of the mercury currently entering U.S. water bodies and contaminating fish is the result of air emissions, which following atmospheric transport, deposit onto watersheds or directly to water bodies."

When power plants burn coal, mercury is released from the coal into the air in three basic forms, including elemental mercury, oxidized mercury, and particulate-bound mercury. Depending on its form, mercury can deposit onto land or water bodies within 50 to 500 miles of its source (oxidized and particulate-bound mercury) or be transported long distances on air masses (elemental mercury).

EPA estimates that 60 percent of the mercury deposited in the U.S. comes from domestic man-made sources; the remaining 40 percent comes from man-made sources outside of the U.S., re-emitted mercury from historic U.S. sources, and natural sources. Nationally, EPA estimates that 33 percent of total U.S. mercury deposition is from U.S. power plants.

It is important to note that this estimate of national deposition obscures the impact of local sources on mercury hot spots, or areas with high levels of mercury deposition. The highest deposition rates in the U.S. occur in the southern Great Lakes, the Ohio Valley, the Northeast, and scattered areas in the South. In regions where deposition is high, local and regional sources are the main cause of elevated mercury concentrations. A 2003 analysis of EPA data found that local sources can account for 50 to 80 percent of mercury deposition at hot spots.

In addition, recent research indicates that elemental mercury emissions from power plants can be rapidly converted to oxidized mercury and deposited locally or regionally as well, suggesting that power plants contribute even more to localized hot spots than previously thought.

Poor Nations Need Alternatives to Fossil Fuels

Christopher Flavin and Molly Hull Aeck

Christopher Flavin is president and Molly Hull Aeck is renewable energy program manager at the Worldwatch Institute, a research organization that analyzes environmental data from around the world to encourage sustainable societies.

Affordable energy services are among the essential ingredients of economic development, including eradication of extreme poverty as called for in the United Nations Millennium Development Goals (MDGs). Meeting these energy needs economically and sustainably requires a balanced energy portfolio that is suited to the economic, social and resource conditions of individual countries and regions. The Renewable Energy Policy Network for the 21st Century (REN21) released a report concluding that in many circumstances, renewable energy sources such as wind, solar, hydro, geothermal and bioenergy have an important role to play, alongside fossil fuels, in an energy portfolio that supports achievement of the MDGs.

The Need for Energy Independence

Roughly 1.6 billion people worldwide do not have access to electricity in their homes, representing slightly more than one quarter of the world population. They often go without refrigeration, radios and even light. The International Energy Agency estimates that if the MDG poverty-reduction target is to be met, modern energy services will need to be provided to an additional 700 million people by 2015.

Chris Flavin and Molly Hull Aeck, "Cleaner, Greener and Richer," *tompaine.com*, September 15, 2005. Reproduced by permission.

In recent decades, the energy needs of poor people have been most often met via petroleum-based liquid fuels, and by extension of the electricity grid, which is powered mainly by fossil fuels and hydropower. However, these conventional energy systems are often out of reach for people in remote areas, and even in urban slums they are sometimes too expensive for the poorest to afford. In addition, in many developing countries, most of the fuel and many of the technologies are imported. Of the 47 poorest countries, 38 are net importers of oil, and 25 import all of their oil.

The economic risk of relying primarily on imported energy has grown in recent years as oil prices have become less stable, doubling in less than two years [between 2003 and 2005] to more than $60 per barrel. These rising prices have had a disproportionate impact on poor people who depend on kerosene and liquefied petroleum gas (LPG) for their basic cooking and heating. In many poor countries, governments subsidize basic fuels such as kerosene, and the cost of these subsidies has skyrocketed [since 2003]—reducing the funds available to governments to pay for education, health care, clean water and other public investments that are essential for meeting the MDGs.

Renewable energy technologies can . . . make indirect contributions to alleviating poverty.

The Benefits of Renewable Energy

The rapid recent growth in solar, wind, geothermal and biomass energy [globally], coupled with ongoing technology improvements and cost reductions, is making a growing array of renewable energy options available to help achieve the MDGs. Although the strongest renewable energy growth has been in grid-connected power systems and liquid fuels for transportation, several renewable energy technologies are well-suited to providing modern energy services for low-income people, including:

- biogas for decentralized cooking and electricity

- small hydro power for local electricity

- small wind power for water pumping and local electricity

- solar photovoltaics for local electricity

- solar collectors for water and space heating

- ethanol and biodiesel for agriculture and transportation

- large hydro power for grid electricity

- large wind power for grid electricity

- geothermal energy for heat and grid electricity

Renewable energy projects implemented in scores of developing countries—many with international donor assistance—have demonstrated that renewable energy can contribute to poverty alleviation directly. These projects provide the energy needed for creating businesses and jobs—turning locally available resources into productive economic assets.

Renewable energy technologies can also make indirect contributions to alleviating poverty by providing energy for cooking and space heating. Improved biomass stoves and liquid and gaseous fuels derived from locally produced biomass can reduce the drain on household income, while freeing up time for education and income-generating activities. By making light more affordable and reliable, renewable energy technologies also permit schools and businesses to operate after dark.

Renewable energy can contribute to education as well, by providing electricity to schools, improving attendance, retaining teachers and powering educational media. Renewable energy for cooking and heating can reduce the time that children, especially girls, spend out of school collecting fuel. In addition, the displacement of traditional fuels reduces the health problems from indoor air pollution produced by burning those fuels. Renewable energy can also contribute to improved health by providing energy to refrigerate medicine, sterilize medical equipment and incinerate medical waste. And it can provide power for supplying the fresh water and sewer services needed to reduce the burden of infectious disease.

Governments Should Invest in Renewables

By developing energy sources such as large hydro power, wind power, geothermal power and liquid biofuels, developing countries can reduce their dependence on oil and natural gas, creating energy portfolios that are less vulnerable to price fluctuations. In many circumstances, these investments can be economically justified as less expensive than a narrower, fossil fuel dominated energy system.

Most poor countries have abundant renewable resources, including varying combinations of solar, wind, geothermal, and biomass, as well as the ability to manufacture the relatively labor-intensive systems that harness these. However, only a few developing countries have adopted the policies needed to spur the development of renewable energy technologies and markets, which have been dominated by Europe, Japan, and North America. The exceptions include Brazil, which has built the world's leading biofuels industry; and China and India, which are leaders in developing decentralized renewable sources such as small hydro, small wind, biogas and solar water heating.

Renewable energy technologies face a number of barriers that have delayed scaling up their production and use in developing countries. Most renewable energy sources require a significant upfront investment, as has been the case for most of the conventional energy sources that dominate today's energy system. This means that in the early years of deployment, renewable energy options are typically more expensive than the conventional alternative. Government intervention to level the playing field is therefore needed to start the development process. Experience shows that as the scale of use increases, costs decline significantly in the early years.

It is through the combined efforts of governments and the private sector that strong, sustained markets for renewable energy are most likely to develop.

World Oil Supplies Are Not Running Out

Daniel Yergin

Daniel Yergin is chairman of Cambridge Energy Research Associates. His book The Prize: The Epic Quest for Oil, Money, and Power *received the Pulitzer Prize.*

We're not running out of oil. Not yet.

"Shortage" is certainly in the air—and in the price. Right now [July 2005] the oil market is tight, even tighter than it was on the eve of the 1973 oil crisis. In this high-risk market, "surprises" ranging from political instability to hurricanes could send oil prices spiking higher. Moreover, the specter of an energy shortage is not limited to oil. Natural gas supplies are not keeping pace with growing demand. Even supplies of coal, which generates about half of the country's electricity, are constrained. . . .

Between 2004 and 2010, capacity to produce oil . . . could grow by 16 million barrels a day.

But it is oil that gets most of the attention. Prices around $60 a barrel, driven by high-demand growth, are fueling the fear of imminent shortage—that the world is going to begin running out of oil in five or 10 years. This shortage, it is argued, will be amplified by the substantial and growing demand from two giants: China and India.

The Growing Oil Supply

Yet this fear is not borne out by the fundamentals of supply. Our new, field-by-field analysis of production capacity, led by my colleagues Peter Jackson and Robert Esser, is quite at odds with the current view and leads to a strikingly different conclusion: There will be a large, unprecedented buildup of oil supply in the next few years. Between 2004 and 2010, capacity to produce oil (not actual production) could grow by 16 million barrels a day—from 85 million barrels per day to 101 million barrels a day—a 20 percent increase. Such growth over the next few years would relieve the current pressure on supply and demand.

Where will this growth come from? It is pretty evenly divided between non-OPEC and OPEC [Organization of Petroleum Exporting Countries]. The largest non-OPEC growth is projected for Canada, Kazakhstan, Brazil, Azerbaijan, Angola and Russia. In the OPEC countries, significant growth is expected to occur in Saudi Arabia, Nigeria, Algeria and Libya, among others. Our estimate for growth in Iraq is quite modest—only 1 million barrels a day—reflecting the high degree of uncertainty there. In the forecast, the United States remains almost level, with development in the deep-water areas of the Gulf of Mexico compensating for declines elsewhere.

While questions can be raised about specific countries, this forecast is not speculative. It is based on what is already unfolding. The oil industry is governed by a "law of long lead times." Much of the new capacity that will become available between now and 2010 is under development. Many of the projects that embody this new capacity were approved in the 2001–03 period, based on price expectations much lower than current prices.

There are risks to any forecast. In this case, the risks are not the "below ground" ones of geology or lack of resources. Rather, they are "above ground" —political instability, outright conflict, terrorism or slowdowns in decision making on the part of governments in oil-producing countries. Yet, even with the scaling back of the forecast, it would still constitute a big increase in output.

Improving Technology

This is not the first time that the world has "run out of oil." It's more like the fifth. Cycles of shortage and surplus characterize the entire history of the oil industry. A similar fear of shortage after World War I was one of the main drivers for cobbling together the three easternmost provinces of the defunct Ottoman Turkish Empire to create Iraq. In more recent times, the "permanent oil shortage" of the 1970s gave way to the glut and price collapse of the 1980s.

But this time, it is said, is "different." A common pattern in the shortage periods is to underestimate the impact of technology. And, once again, technology is key. "Proven [oil] reserves" are not necessarily a good guide to the future. The current Securities and Exchange Commission disclosure rules, which define "reserves" for investors, are based on 30-year-old technology and offer an incomplete picture of future potential. As skills improve, output from many producing regions will be much greater than anticipated. The share of "unconventional oil"—Canadian oil sands, ultra-deep-water developments, "natural gas liquids"—will rise from 10 percent of total capacity in 1990 to 30 percent by 2010. The "unconventional" will cease being frontier and will instead become "conventional." Over the next few years, new facilities will be transforming what are inaccessible natural gas reserves in different parts of the world into a quality, diesel-like fuel.

The growing supply of energy should not lead us to underestimate the longer-term challenge of providing energy for a growing world economy. At this point, even with greater efficiency, it looks as though the world could be using 50 percent more oil 25 years from now. That is a very big challenge. But at least for the next several years, the growing production capacity will take the air out of the fear of imminent shortage. And that in turn will provide us the breathing space to address the investment needs and the full panoply of technologies and approaches—from development to conservation—that will be required to fuel a growing world economy, ensure energy security and meet the needs of what is becoming the global middle class.

The Threat of Global Warming Is Exaggerated

Jack M. Hollander

Jack M. Hollander, author of The Real Environmental Crisis: Why Poverty, Not Affluence, Is the Environment's Number One Enemy, *from which this viewpoint is excerpted, is professor emeritus of energy and resources at the University of California at Berkeley.*

Although the debate over human impacts on climate probably won't be resolved for decades, a case can be made for adopting a less alarmist view of a warmer world. In any case, the warmer world is already here. Look at the historical evidence on the effects of temperature change. In the last twenty-five hundred years, global temperatures have varied by more than three degrees Centigrade, and some of the changes have been much more abrupt than the gradual changes projected by the IPCC [United Nations Intergovernmental Panel on Climate Change]. During all of recorded history humans have survived and prospered in climate zones that differ from each other far more than the changes in global temperatures now being discussed. Today people show a definite preference for warmer climates. In the United States, one of the few places where environmental migration is possible within the same political entity, the migration from the cold Northeast to the warm Southwest is far greater than the reverse flow.

It is not unreasonable to surmise that global warming could be beneficial to agriculture.

Jack M. Hollander, *The Real Environmental Crisis: Why Poverty, Not Affluence Is the Environment's Number One Enemy,* Berkeley: University of California Press, 2003. Copyright © 2003 by The Regents of the University of California. Reproduced by permission.

No Need for Alarm

Those who predict agricultural losses from a warmer climate have most likely got it backwards. Warm periods have historically benefited the development of civilization, and cold periods have been detrimental. For example, the Medieval Warm Period, from about 900 to 1300, facilitated the Viking settlements of Iceland and Greenland, whereas the subsequent Little Ice Age led to crop failures, famines, and disease. Even a small temperature increase brings a longer and more frost-free growing season—a definite advantage for many farmers, especially those in large cold countries such as Russia and Canada. Enrichment of atmospheric CO_2 [carbon dioxide, the main gas associated with global warming] is well-known by agronomists to stimulate plant growth and development in greenhouses; thus such enrichment at the global level can be expected to lead to an increase in global vegetative or biological productivity, as well as an increase in water-use efficiency. Since a warmer climate resulting from atmospheric CO_2 enrichment would improve plants as biological converters of solar energy, it is not unreasonable to surmise that global warming could be beneficial to agriculture. Studies of this issue from an economic perspective have reached the same conclusion: moderate global warming would most likely produce net economic benefits, raising gross national product and average income, especially for the agriculture and forestry sectors. Such projections of the future, of course, are subject to great uncertainty and cannot exclude the possibility that unexpected negative impacts would occur.

Concerns have been raised that warmer temperatures would spread insect-borne diseases such as malaria, dengue fever, and yellow fever through increased precipitation leading to expansion of favorable habitats. There is no solid evidence for this concern. These illnesses were common in North America, Western Europe, and Russia during the nineteenth century, when the world was colder than it is today. Although the spread of disease is a complex matter, the main carriers of these diseases are most likely humans traveling the globe and insects traveling with people and goods. The main allies against future disease are surely not cold climates but rather improvements in regional insect control, water quality, and public health. . . .

The question . . . is whether ongoing sea-level rise has anything to do with human use of fossil fuels.

Are Sea Levels Rising?

One of the direst (and most highly publicized) predictions of global warming theorists is that greenhouse gas warming will cause sea level to rise and that as a result many oceanic islands and lowland areas, such as Bangladesh, may be submerged. But in fact, sea level is rising now and has been rising for thousands of years, once having been low enough to expose a land bridge between Siberia and Alaska over which humans walked in their migrations from Asia to North America. Recent analyses suggest that sea level rose at a rate of about one to two centimeters per century (0.4 to 0.8 inches) over the last three thousand years. Direct sea-level measurements made throughout the twentieth century have been interpreted in some studies to show that the level is presently rising at a much faster rate, about ten to twenty-five centimeters per century (4 to 10 inches), but other studies conclude that the rate is much lower than this. To whatever extent sea-level rise may have accelerated, the change is thought to have taken place before the period of industrialization.

The question is, of course, whether the ongoing sea-level rise has anything to do with human use of fossil fuels. Before looking at that, however, let's take a step back and ask what science has to say about how global temperature change may relate to sea level change. This is more complicated than it first appears. One factor is that water expands as it warms, which would contribute to *rising* sea level. A factor that could work in the opposite direction is that warming increases evaporation of ocean water, which could increase the snowfall on the Arctic and Antarctic ice sheets, removing water from the ocean and *lowering* sea level. The relative importance of these two factors is not known. We do know from studies of the West Antarctic Ice Sheet that this ice sheet has been melting continuously since the last great ice age, about twenty thousand years ago, and that sea level has been rising ever since. Continued melting of this ice sheet until the next ice age may be inevitable, in which case sea level would rise by fifteen to eighteen feet when the sheet is completely melted. Other mechanisms have been suggested for natural sea-level rise, including tectonic changes in the shape of the ocean basins. The theoretical computer climate models attribute most of the sea-level rise to thermal expansion of the oceans, and thus they predict that further global temperature increase (presumably from human activities) will accelerate the ongoing sea-level rise. Since these models are unable, however, to deal adequately with the totality of natural phenomena involved, their predictions about sea-level rise should be viewed skeptically.

Humans Will Adapt

The natural causes of sea-level rise, such as those just mentioned, are part of the earth's evolution. They have nothing to do with human activities, and there is nothing that humans can do about them. Civilization has always adjusted to such changes just as it has adjusted to earthquakes and other natural phenomena over which humans have no control. This is not to say that adjusting to natural changes is not sometimes painful; certainly, adjusting to earthquakes and tornadoes is very painful. But if there is nothing we can do about certain natural phenomena, we do adjust, whether it is painful or not. Sea-level rise is most likely a phenomenon over which humans have no control.

As to the unfortunate flood victims in vulnerable low-lying areas such as Bangladesh, they should be assisted by the international community out of humanitarian considerations regardless of the causes of their frequent flood disasters. Such assistance should in no way be tied to the vicissitudes of political or scientific debate over complex subjects such as global warming or ice-sheet melting.

Another claim of some environmentalists is that weather-related natural disasters, including hurricanes, tornadoes, droughts, and floods, have been increasing in frequency and severity presumably as the result of human-caused global warming. The actual historical record does not support such claims. On the contrary, several recent statistical studies have found that natural disasters, including hurricanes, typhoons, tropical storms, floods, blizzards, wildfires, heat waves, and earthquakes, have not been increasing in frequency. The *costs* of losses from natural disasters are indeed rising, to the dismay of insurance companies and government emergency agencies, but this is because people in the affluent societies have increasingly constructed expensive properties in areas vulnerable to natural hazards, such as coastlines, steep hills, and forested areas. They continue to do so not only because such areas often provide the most attractive sites for habitation but also because the costs of disaster insurance are spread over the larger society and thus are relatively low to the insured.

The overall cost of the worst-case consequences of warming would be no more than about a 2 percent reduction in world output.

The True Cost of Action

Since society has choices, one should ask what would be the likely effects if, on one hand, people decided to adjust to climate change, regardless of its causes, or on the other, governments implemented drastic policies to attempt to lessen the presumed human contribution to the change. At least from an economic perspective, adjusting to the change would almost surely be the winner. Several analyses have projected that the overall cost of the worst-case consequences of warming would be no more than about a 2 percent reduction in world output. Since average per-capita income will probably quadruple during the next century, the potential loss seems small indeed. A more recent economic study emphasizing adaptation to climate change indicates that in the market economy of the United States the overall impacts of modest global warming are likely to be beneficial rather than damaging. The amount of net benefit is small, about 0.2 percent of the economy. (One must always keep in mind the statistical uncertainties inherent in such analyses; i.e., there are small probabilities that the benefits or costs could turn out to be much greater than or much less than the most probable outcomes.)

In contrast, the economic costs of governmental actions ("insurance" policies) restricting the use of fossil fuels could be large. . . . One U.S. government study suggested that a cost-effective way of bringing about fossil-fuel reductions would be a combination of carbon taxes and international trading in emissions rights. Emissions rights trading was in fact included in the modified Kyoto agreement [on greenhouse-gas reduction]. Such trading schemes would result in huge income transfers as rich nations pay poor nations for emissions quotas that the latter would probably not have used anyway. It is not reasonable to assume that the rich nations would be willing to do this.

Taking into account the large uncertainties in estimating the future growth of the world economy and corresponding growth in fossil-fuel use, one group of economists estimates that the costs of greenhouse-gas reduction would be in the neighborhood of 1 percent of world output, while another estimate is higher, around 5 percent of output. The costs would be expected to be considerably higher if large reductions were forced upon the global economy over a short time period or if the most economically efficient schemes to bring about the reductions were not actually employed—a likely possibility. Political economists [Henry D.] Jacoby, [Ronald G.] Prinn, and [Richard] Schmalensee put it more strongly: "It will be nearly impossible to slow climate warming [sic] appreciably without condemning much of the world to poverty, unless energy sources that emit little or no carbon dioxide become competitive with conventional fossil fuels."

If it turns out that human activity is adding to the natural warming, the amount will probably be small, and society can adjust.

A Wiser Course of Action

So what is my bottom line about global warming? First, some warming has been underway for over a century, at least partly from natural causes, and the world has been adjusting to it as it did with past climate changes. Second, if it turns out that human activity is adding to the natural warming, the amount will probably be small, and society can adjust to that as well, at relatively low cost or even net benefit. Third, the industrial nations are not likely to carry out inefficient, Kyoto-type mandated reductions in fossil-fuel use on the basis of so incomplete a scientific foundation as presently exists. The costs of following the "precautionary principle" in this way could well exceed the potential benefits. Far more effective would be policies and actions by the industrial countries to accelerate the development, in the near term, of technologies that utilize fossil fuels (and all resources) more efficiently and, in the longer term, technologies that do not require use of fossil fuels.

Finally, the industrial nations should ensure the future credibility of climate science by totally separating the pursuit of this important science from global politics. The affluent countries should continue to support strong climate-research programs, which will improve the theoretical understanding of and empirical database on factors that influence long-term climate change, and also increase understanding of short-term weather dynamics. Such research not only is relevant to the greenhouse-gas issue but also will richly reward humankind by improving people's ability to cope with extreme weather events such as hurricanes, tornadoes, and floods, whatever their causes.

Improved Technologies Make Coal a Clean Fuel

U.S. Department of Energy

The U.S. Department of Energy's Office of Fossil Energy is responsible for several high-priority presidential initiatives, including implementation of the George W. Bush administration's $2 billion, 10-year initiative to develop a new generation of environmentally sound clean coal technologies.

Coal is our most abundant fossil fuel. The United States has more coal than the rest of the world has oil. There is still enough coal underground in this country to provide energy for the next 200 to 300 years.

But coal is not a perfect fuel.

Trapped inside coal are traces of impurities like sulfur and nitrogen. When coal burns, these impurities are released into the air.

While floating in the air, these substances can combine with water vapor (for example, in clouds) and form droplets that fall to earth as weak forms of sulfuric and nitric acid—scientists call it "acid rain."

We have technology that can filter out 99 percent of the tiny particles and remove more than 95 percent of the acid rain pollutants in coal.

There are also tiny specks of minerals—including common dirt—mixed in coal. These tiny particles don't burn and make up the ash left behind in a coal combustor. Some of the tiny particles also get caught up in the swirling combustion

U.S. Department of Energy, Office of Fossil Energy, "Cleaning Up Coal," fossil.energy. gov, August 1, 2005.

gases and, along with water vapor, form the smoke that comes out of a coal plant's smokestack. Some of these particles are so small that 30 of them laid side-by-side would barely equal the width of a human hair!

Coal and Carbon Dioxide

Also, coal, like all fossil fuels, is formed out of carbon. All living things—even people—are made up of carbon. . . .But when coal burns, its carbon combines with oxygen in the air and forms carbon dioxide. Carbon dioxide is a colorless, odorless gas, but in the atmosphere, it is one of several gases that can trap the earth's heat. Many scientists believe this is causing the earth's temperature to rise, and this warming could be altering the earth's climate. . . .

Sounds like coal is a dirty fuel to burn. Many years ago, it was. But things have changed. Especially in the last 20 years, scientists have developed ways to capture the pollutants trapped in coal before the impurities can escape into the atmosphere. Today, we have technology that can filter out 99 percent of the tiny particles and remove more than 95 percent of the acid rain pollutants in coal.

We also have new technologies that cut back on the release of carbon dioxide by burning coal more efficiently. . . .

Most modern power plants . . . are required to have special devices installed that clean the sulfur from the coal's combustion gases.

How Do You Make Coal Cleaner?

Actually there are several ways.

Take sulfur, for example. Sulfur is a yellowish substance that exists in tiny amounts in coal. In some coals found in Ohio, Pennsylvania, West Virginia and other eastern states, sulfur makes up from 3 to 10 percent of the weight of coal. . . .

One way is to clean the coal before it arrives at the power plant. One of the ways this is done is by simply crushing the coal into small chunks and washing it. Some of the sulfur that exists in tiny specks in coal (called "pyritic sulfur" because it is combined with iron to form iron pyrite, otherwise known as "fool's gold") can be washed out of the coal in this manner. Typically, in one washing process, the coal chunks are fed into a large water-filled tank. The coal floats to the surface while the sulfur impurities sink. There are facilities around the country called "coal preparation plants" that clean coal this way. . . .

Most modern power plants—and all plants built after 1978—are required to have special devices installed that clean the sulfur from the coal's combustion gases before the gases go up the smokestack. The technical name for these devices is "flue gas desulfurization units," but most people just call them "scrubbers"—because they "scrub" the sulfur out of the smoke released by coal-burning boilers. . . .

One of the best ways to prevent [nitrogen oxide emissions] is to prevent it from forming in the first place.

Removing NO_x from Coal

Nitrogen is the most common part of the air we breathe. In fact, about 80% of the air is nitrogen. Normally, nitrogen atoms float around joined to each other like chemical couples. But when air is heated—in a coal boiler's flame, for example— these nitrogen atoms break apart and join with oxygen. This forms "nitrogen oxides"—or, as it is sometimes called, "NO_x," (rhymes with "socks"). NO_x can also be formed from the atoms of nitrogen that are trapped inside coal.

In the air, NO_x is a pollutant. It can cause smog, the brown haze you sometimes see around big cities. It is also one of the pollutants that forms "acid rain." And it can help form something called "groundlevel ozone," another type of pollutant that can make the air dingy.

NO_x can be produced by any fuel that burns hot enough. Automobiles, for example, produce NO_x when they burn gasoline. But a lot of NO_x comes from coal-burning power plants, so the Clean Coal Technology Program developed new ways to reduce this pollutant.

One of the best ways to reduce NO_x is to prevent it from forming in the first place. Scientists have found ways to burn coal (and other fuels) in burners where there is more fuel than air in the hottest combustion chambers. Under these conditions, most of the oxygen in air combines with the fuel, rather than with the nitrogen. The burning mixture is then sent into a second combustion chamber where a similar process is repeated until all the fuel is burned.

This concept is called "staged combustion" because coal is burned in stages. A new family of coal burners called "low-NO_x burners" has been developed using this way of burning coal. These burners can reduce the amount of NO_x released into the air by more than half. Today, because of research and the Clean Coal Technology Program, more than half of all the large coal-burning boilers in the United States will be using these types of burners. By the year 2000, more than 3 out of every 4 boilers [was] outfitted with these new clean coal technologies.

There is also a family of new technologies that work like "scrubbers" by cleaning NO_x from the flue gases (the smoke) of coal burners. Some of these devices use special chemicals called "catalysts" that break apart the NO_x into non-polluting gases. Although these devices are more expensive than "low-NO_x burners," they can remove up to 90 percent of NO_x pollutants.

But in the future, there may be an even cleaner way to burn coal in a power plant. Or maybe, there may be a way that doesn't burn the coal at all.

A "Bed" for Burning Coal?

It was a wet, chilly day in Washington DC in 1979 when a few scientists and engineers joined with government and college officials on the campus of Georgetown University to celebrate the completion of one of the world's most advanced coal combustors.

It was a small coal burner by today's standards, but large enough to provide heat and steam for much of the university campus. But the new boiler built beside the campus tennis courts was unlike most other boilers in the world.

It was called a "fluidized bed boiler." In a typical coal boiler, coal would be crushed into very fine particles, blown into the boiler, and ignited to form a long, lazy flame. Or in other types of boilers, the burning coal would rest on grates. But in a "fluidized bed boiler," crushed coal particles float inside the boiler, suspended on upward-blowing jets of air. The red-hot mass of floating coal—called the "bed"—would bubble and tumble around like boiling lava inside a volcano. Scientists call this being "fluidized." That's how the name "fluidized bed boiler" came about. . . .

A fluidized bed boiler can burn very dirty coal and remove 90% or more of the sulfur and nitrogen pollutants.

A Cleaner Way to Burn Coal

Why does a fluidized bed boiler burn coal cleaner? There are two major reasons. One, the tumbling action allows limestone to be mixed in with the coal. . . . Limestone is a sulfur sponge—it absorbs sulfur pollutants. As coal burns in a fluidized bed boiler, it releases sulfur. But just as rapidly, the limestone tumbling around beside the coal captures the sulfur. A chemical reaction occurs, and the sulfur gases are changed into a dry powder, that can be removed from the boiler. (This dry powder—called *calcium sulfate*—can be processed into the wallboard we use for building walls inside our houses.)

The second reason a fluidized bed boiler burns cleaner is that it burns "cooler." Now, cooler in this sense is still pretty hot—about 1400 degrees F. But older coal boilers operate at temperatures nearly twice that (almost 3000 degrees F). Remember NO_x? NO_x forms when a fuel burns hot enough to break apart nitrogen molecules in the air and cause the nitrogen atoms to join with oxygen atoms. But 1400 degrees isn't hot enough for that to happen, so very little NO_x forms in a fluidized bed boiler.

The result is that a fluidized bed boiler can burn very dirty coal and remove 90% or more of the sulfur and nitrogen pollutants while the coal is burning. Fluidized bed boilers can also burn just about anything else—wood, ground-up railroad ties, even soggy coffee grounds.

Today, fluidized bed boilers are operating or being built that are 10 to 20 times larger than the small unit built almost 20 years ago at Georgetown University. There are more than 300 of these boilers around this country and the world. The Clean Coal Technology Program helped test these boilers in Colorado, in Ohio and, most recently, in Florida.

Improving Technology

A new type of fluidized bed boiler makes a major improvement in the basic system. It encases the entire boiler inside a large pressure vessel, much like the pressure cooker used in homes for canning fruits and vegetables—except the ones used in power plants are the size of a small house! Burning coal in a "pressurized fluidized bed boiler" produces a high-pressure stream of combustion gases that can spin a gas turbine to make electricity, then boil water for a steam turbine— two sources of electricity from the same fuel!

A "pressurized fluidized bed boiler" is a more efficient way to burn coal. In fact, future boilers using this system will be able to generate 50% more electricity from coal than a regular power plant from the same amount of coal. That's like getting 3 units of power when you used to get only 2.

Because it uses less fuel to produce the same amount of power, a more efficient "pressurized fluidized bed boiler" will reduce the amount of carbon dioxide (a greenhouse gas) released from coal-burning power plants.

"Pressurized fluidized bed boilers" are one of the newest ways to burn coal cleanly. But there is another new way that doesn't actually burn the coal at all.

Gas from Coal

Don't think of coal as a solid black rock. Think of it as a mass of atoms. Most of the atoms are carbon. A few are hydrogen. And there are some others, like sulfur and nitrogen, mixed in. Chemists can take this mass of atoms, break it apart, and make new substances—like gas!

How do you break apart the atoms of coal? You may think it would take a sledgehammer, but actually all it takes is water and heat. Heat coal hot enough inside a big metal vessel, blast it with steam (the water), and it breaks apart. Into what?

The carbon atoms join with oxygen that is in the air (or pure oxygen can be injected into the vessel). The hydrogen atoms join with each other. The result is a mixture of carbon monoxide and hydrogen—a gas.

You can burn it and use the hot combustion gases to spin a gas turbine to generate electricity. The exhaust gases coming out of the gas turbine are hot enough to boil water to make steam that can spin another type of turbine to generate even more electricity. But why go to all the trouble to turn the coal into gas if all you are going to do is burn it?

A major reason is that the impurities in coal—like sulfur, nitrogen and many other trace elements—can be almost entirely filtered out when coal is changed into a gas (a process called *gasification*). In fact, scientists have ways to remove

99.9% of the sulfur and small dirt particles from the coal gas. Gasifying coal is one of the best ways to clean pollutants out of it.

Another reason is that the coal gases—carbon monoxide and hydrogen—don't have to be burned. They can also be used as valuable chemicals. Scientists have developed chemical reactions that turn carbon monoxide and hydrogen into everything from liquid fuels for cars and trucks to plastic toothbrushes!

Fossil Fuels Will Help Relieve Global Poverty

Philip Stott

Philip Stott is professor emeritus of biogeography at the University of London.

You are a tribal woman in the Jharkhand region of northeastern India. Sustaining life has always been tough, but it has become harder of late. Environmentalists, obsessed by what they see as the deforestation of the [Indian] subcontinent, have imposed a fuel-cutting ban in the protected forest near your village.

It was bad enough for your mother, who had to spend hours bending down, hacking saplings with her small sickle-shaped *daoli*, but now you can only gather dry, fallen leaves or small twigs from the thorny bush you call *putus*. You must also go much farther afield to collect your daily fuel needs.

Small cooking fires have been blamed for causing a brown haze above Asia that is said to be threatening the rich countries of Europe.

The Energy Poor

Yet you are probably unaware that you live in a potentially wealthy and powerful country, one with a nuclear deterrent and one that produces some of the finest writers and scientists in the world. You would be even more surprised to learn that your small cooking fires have been blamed for causing a brown haze above Asia that is said to be threatening the rich countries of Europe with dire climate change.

You may also find it amusing, if somewhat paradoxical, to discover that your leaves and twigs are called "biomass fuels", and that biomass fuels are being touted as part of a "green" solution to save the world. And you would be amazed that this week [in August 2002] more than 60,000 people are sitting down in Johannesburg, South Africa, at a United Nations' World Summit on Sustainable Development, the "Earth Summit 2002", to discuss both you and the planet.

But, "unknown citizen", you are not alone. While food is more affordable for most, you are one of the three billion people who must survive on less than £2 [about $3] a day. Overall, the average expectancy of life at birth has doubled during the past two centuries, although you know personally some of the 800 million who are chronically undernourished.

And you share with 1.3 billion a lack of access to safe, clean drinking water, so that two million people, mainly children, die each year of water-borne diseases. But, above all, along with a quarter of the world's population, you have no supply of power or electricity for your daily needs. You must laboriously garner and burn dung or wood to heat your hearth, light your darkness, and cook your food. You are one of the energy poor.

Freedom Through Fossil Fuels

In *The Ultimate Resource 2*, Julian Simon describes energy as the "master resource", and he argues that "if the cost of usable energy is low enough, all other important resources can be made plentiful". For the past 200 years, this master resource has been energy derived from hydrocarbons—from coal, oil and gas.

Although at first taking a toll through miners' lives, this energy eventually freed from drudgery our European fuel gatherers, the equivalents of our "unknown citizen." . . . If the

Earth Summit does nothing to liberate the Asian and African fuel gatherers from their burdens, then it will have failed abysmally.

But, unfortunately, energy could prove to be one of the most contentious issues at the summit, because environmentalists have decreed hydrocarbons to be the new witchcraft behind "global warming" and "unsustainability", despite the fact, so well argued by Robert L. Bradley, Jr., in a new book, *Sustainable Development: Promoting Progress or Perpetuating Poverty?*, that the hydrocarbon age is in its infancy.

Even the Intergovernmental Panel on Climate Change (IPCC) has calculated that total cumulative world consumption of hydrocarbons constitutes only 1.4 per cent of what is thought to remain. Moreover, new members of the hydrocarbon family are coming on-stream, such as the so-called "fourth fossil fuel", Orimulsion, a tar-like oil the estimated reserves of which are greater than the global supply of crude oil on an energy-equivalent basis.

And yet further, there is the increasing flexibility of hydrocarbons, which is augmenting significantly the amount of economically recoverable material, as with natural gas. But environmentalists do not want hydrocarbons. They advocate instead "renewable energy", while at the same time opposing the very renewable energy projects they propose.

With more than a quarter of the world's population classed as 'energy poor', we must have growth in energy use.

Renewable Energy Is Not the Answer

Hydroelectric power is rejected because it involves the resettlement of local people, interrupts fish migration, and causes loss of habitat. Wind farms are rightly attacked because they destroy some of the last remaining wilderness and can kill birds. Tidal barrages disrupt estuarine ecosystems, while geothermal projects mar sensitive ecological areas.

Yet other "renewables" remain more fantasy than reality, with most photovoltaic solar cells, for example, producing less energy in their lifetime than is needed to make them in the first place. Big alternatives, such as nuclear fission and fusion, are, of course, rejected out of hand.

With more than a quarter of the world's population classed as "energy poor", we must have growth in energy use. And, just as economic growth has removed the heavy burden from the wood gatherer, so too it must be allowed, unfettered by environmental myths, to replace the leaves, twigs and choking smoke of millions of fires.

And what of the Asian brown haze that has so suddenly been brought to our attention? Known already in the early 1980s by U.S. pilots flying out of their base at Diego Garcia, this haze has probably been around for hundreds of years, fed by the fires of our "unknown citizen" and of the billions who have lived before her on the great Asian continent.

This is therefore a plea for our "unknown citizen", knowledge of whose life is based on the outstanding work of Dr Sarah Jewitt of Nottingham University. Blessed are the poor in energy, for they, like us, will become rich in hydrocarbons. Blessed are the poor in water, for they shall drink safely, while we, worried about every shadow of a chemical, spend millions on "natural" bottled water because we no longer like the tap water that has made us healthy and saved so many lives.

CHAPTER 2

Do Alternative Energy Sources Benefit the Environment?

Chapter Preface

If using conventional energy sources such as coal, oil, and natural gas did not create pollution, there likely would be no debate about using alternative energy sources. But the unfortunate fact is that fossil-fuel use creates greenhouse gases that many scientists believe cause global warming. To address the problem, many experts argue that nations should transition to clean, renewable energy. Indeed, many consider alternative energy synonymous with clean energy.

But is it necessarily the case that alternatives are better for the environment than are conventional sources? Hydrogen fuel cells are a case in point. Hydrogen fuel cells create no pollution because they do not burn fuel in the traditional sense but combine hydrogen and oxygen to release energy. A car running on hydrogen emits nothing more than water from its tailpipe. However, usable hydrogen does not exist anywhere on earth. It must be made using one of several processes, such as electrolysis (splitting water molecules into hydrogen and oxygen), all of which require energy. To date, most of this energy comes from fossil fuels; thus the creation of clean hydrogen, at least for now, necessitates the use of dirty fossil fuels. Says John Heywood, director of the Massachusetts Institute of Technology's Sloan Automotive Laboratory, "If the hydrogen does not come from renewable sources, then it is simply not worth doing, environmentally or economically."

Producing usable hydrogen from renewables, however, has proven problematic. The main obstacle is that renewables such as wind and solar power do not contain nearly the same amount of energy as do fossil fuels. Thus, to make a certain quantity of hydrogen using alternatives would take more energy than it would to make the same quantity using coal. Consequently, hydrogen produced from renewables is expensive. Plans to produce hydrogen using nuclear power have also drawn fire, with critics arguing that increasing nuclear energy usage will create unacceptable amounts of radioactive waste.

Hydrogen is often touted as the energy of the future because in itself it is an abundant and clean energy source but, as mentioned, has its own environmental drawbacks. Authors in the following chapter explore the environmental impacts of several alternative energy sources. The viewpoints make clear that finding the perfect power source to fuel modern economies without harming the environment is enormously challenging.

Nuclear Power Benefits the Environment

Patrick Moore

Patrick Moore was a founding member of the environmental organization Greenpeace. He is currently the chairman and chief scientist of Greenspirit Strategies Ltd., a communications consulting firm that delivers strategic planning for sustainability.

I believe the majority of environmental activists . . . have now become so blinded by their extremist policies that they fail to consider the enormous and obvious benefits of harnessing nuclear power to meet and secure America's growing energy needs.

These benefits far outweigh the risks.

There is now a great deal of scientific evidence showing nuclear power to be an environmentally sound and safe choice.

The Current Situation

Today nuclear energy supplies 20 percent of U.S. electrical energy.

Yet demand for electricity continues to rise and in the coming decades may increase by 50 percent over current levels.

If nothing is done to revitalize the U.S. nuclear industry, the industry's contribution to meeting U.S. energy demands could drop from 20 percent to 9 percent.

What sources of energy would make up the difference?

It is virtually certain that the only technically feasible path is an even greater reliance on fossil fuels.

Patrick Moore, "Testimony Before the U.S. House Subcommittee on Energy and Resources," *Nuclear News*, June 2005. Reproduced by permission of Patrick Moore.

In a "business as usual" scenario, a significant reduction in greenhouse gas (GHG) emissions seems unlikely given our continued heavy reliance on fossil fuels. An investment in nuclear energy would go a long way to reducing this reliance and could actually result in reduced CO_2 emissions from power generation.

According to the Clean Air Council, annual power plant emissions are responsible for 36 percent of carbon dioxide (CO_2), 64 percent of sulfur dioxide (SO_2), 26 percent of nitrogen oxides (NO_x), and 33 percent of mercury emissions (Hg).

These four pollutants cause significant environmental impact, including acid rain, smog, respiratory illness, [and] mercury contamination, and are the major contributors to GHG emissions.

Among power plants, old coal-fired plants produce the majority of these pollutants. By contrast, nuclear power plants produce an insignificant quantity of these pollutants.

According to the Clean Air Council, while 58 percent of power plant boilers in operation in the U.S. are fueled by coal, they contribute 93 percent of NO_x, 96 percent of SO_2, 88 percent of CO_2, and 99 percent of the mercury emitted by the entire power industry.

Prominent environmental figures . . . have now all stated their strong support for nuclear energy.

Prominent Environmentalists See Nuclear Energy as a Solution

Prominent environmental figures like Stewart Brand, founder of the *Whole Earth Catalog*, Gaia theorist James Lovelock, and Hugh Montefiore, former Friends of the Earth leader, have now all stated their strong support for nuclear energy as a practical means of reducing greenhouse gas emissions while meeting the world's increasing energy demands.

I too place myself squarely in that category.

U.K. [United Kingdom] environmentalist James Lovelock, who posited the Gaia theory that the Earth operates as a giant, self-regulating super-organism, now sees nuclear energy as key to our planet's future health. "Civilization is in imminent danger," he warns, "and has to use nuclear—the one safe, available energy source—or suffer the pain soon to be inflicted by our outraged planet."

While I may not be quite so strident as my friend James Lovelock, it is clear that whatever risk there is from increased CO_2 levels in the atmosphere—and there may be considerable risk—can be offset by an emphasis on nuclear energy.

In a recent edition of the Massachusetts Institute of Technology's *Technology Review*, Stewart Brand writes that nuclear energy's problems can be overcome, and that:

> The industry is mature, with a half-century of experience and ever improved engineering behind it. Problematic early reactors like the ones at Three Mile Island and Chernobyl can be supplanted by new, smaller-scale meltdown-proof reactors. . . .Nuclear power plants are very high yield, with low-cost fuel. Finally, they offer the best avenue to a "hydrogen economy," combining high energy and high heat in one place for optimal hydrogen generation.

Nuclear power is already a proven alternative to fossil fuels.

Nuclear Energy Is a Proven Alternative

Indeed, nuclear power is already a proven alternative to fossil fuels.

The United States relies on nuclear power for some 20 percent of its electricity production, and produces nearly one-third of global nuclear energy.

Despite its current limited supply, nuclear energy now provides the vast majority (76.2 percent) of the U.S.'s emission-free generation. (Others include hydroelectric, geothermal, wind, biomass, and solar.)

In 2002, the use of nuclear energy helped the U.S. avoid the release of 189.5 million tons of carbon into the air, if this electricity had been produced by coal.

In fact, the electric sector's carbon emissions would have been 29 percent higher without nuclear power.

And while hydro, geothermal, and wind energy all form an important part of reducing our reliance on fossil fuels, without nuclear energy that reliance will likely not diminish. In 2002, carbon emissions avoided by nuclear power were 1.7 times larger than those avoided by all renewables combined.

A doubling of nuclear energy production would make it possible to significantly reduce total [greenhouse gas] emissions nationwide.

But let me make it clear at this point that I believe there should also be a much greater emphasis on renewable energy production. I believe the two most important renewable energy technologies are wind energy, which has great potential, and ground-source heat pumps, known as geothermal or GeoExchange. Solar panels will not be cost-effective for mass application until their cost is reduced by 5–10 times. I would not be inclined to support an energy policy that focused exclusively on nuclear but would rather insist that an equal emphasis be placed on renewables, even though it is not possible, given present technologies, that renewables could produce the same quantity of power as nuclear plants.

Nuclear energy has already made a sizeable contribution to the reduction of GHG emissions in the U.S.

But more must be done and nuclear energy is pointing the way.

A revitalized American nuclear energy industry, producing an additional 10,000 MW [megawatts] from power plant upgrades, plant restarts, and productivity gains, could assist the electric sector to avoid the emission of 22 millon metric tons of carbon per year by 2012 according to the Nuclear Energy Institute—that's 21 percent of the President's GHG intensity reduction goal.

A doubling of nuclear energy production would make it possible to significantly reduce total GHG emissions nationwide.

While current investment in America's nuclear energy industry languishes, development of commercial plants in other parts of the world is gathering momentum.

In order to create a better environmental and energy-secure future, the U.S. must once again renew its leadership in this area.

Power Plant Safety

As Stewart Brand and other forward-thinking environmentalists and scientists have made clear, technology has now progressed to the point where the activist fear-mongering about the safety of nuclear energy bears no resemblance to reality.

The Chernobyl and Three Mile Island reactors, often raised as examples of nuclear catastrophe by activists, were very different from today's rigorously safe nuclear energy technology. Chernobyl was actually an accident waiting to happen—bad design, shoddy construction, poor maintenance, and unprofessional operation all combined to cause the only terrible accident in reactor history. In my view, the Chernobyl accident was the exception that proves the rule that nuclear reactors are generally safe. Three Mile Island was actually a success story in that the radiation from the partially melted core was contained by the concrete containment structure; it did the job it was designed to do.

Today, approximately one-third of the cost of a nuclear reactor is dedicated to safety systems and infrastructure.

The Chernobyl reactor, for example, was not outfitted with the fully automated, multiple levels of safety and redundancy required for North American reactors.

As we speak there are over 100 nuclear reactors in the U.S. and over 400 worldwide that are producing electricity every day without serious incident.

The fact that reactors produce nuclear waste is often used to support opposition to them. First, there is no technical obstacle to keeping nuclear waste from entering the environment at harmful levels. Second, this is already being accomplished at hundreds of nuclear power sites around the world. It is simply an issue of secure containment and maintenance. Most important, the spent fuel from reactors still has over 95 percent of its potential energy contained within it. Therefore, spent fuel should not be disposed of, it should be stored securely so that in the future we can use this energy productively.

Nuclear reactors produce plutonium that can be extracted and manufactured into nuclear weapons. This is unfortunate but is not in itself justification for eliminating nuclear energy. It appears that the main technologies that have resulted in combat deaths in recent years are machetes, rifles, and car bombs. No one would seriously suggest banning machetes, guns, cars, or the fertilizer and diesel that explosives are made from. Nuclear proliferation must be addressed as a separate policy issue from the production of nuclear energy.

Other Benefits

Besides reductions in GHG emissions and the shift away from our reliance on fossil fuels, nuclear energy offers two important additional and environmentally friendly benefits.

First, nuclear power offers an important and practical pathway to the proposed "hydrogen economy." Unfortunately, there are no hydrogen mines where we can source this element directly. It must be manufactured, from fossil fuels, biomass, or by splitting water into hydrogen and oxygen. Splitting water is the only nongreenhouse gas-emitting approach to manufacturing hydrogen.

Hydrogen, as a fuel, offers the promise of clean, green energy for our automobiles and transportation fleets.

Automobile manufacturers continue to improve hydrogen fuel cells, and the technology may, in the not-too-distant future, become feasible for mass application.

By using electricity, or by using heat directly from nuclear reactors to produce hydrogen, it may be possible to move from fossil fuels for transport energy to using clean hydrogen, thus virtually eliminating smog caused by autos, trucks, and trains.

A hydrogen fuel cell–powered transport fleet would not only virtually eliminate CO_2 emissions, but would eliminate the energy security problem posed by reliance on oil from overseas.

Second, around the world, nuclear energy could be used to solve another growing crisis: the increasing shortage of fresh water available for human consumption and crop irrigation.

By using nuclear energy, seawater could be desalinized to satisfy the ever-growing demand for fresh water without the CO_2 emissions caused by fossil fuel–powered plants.

The Time for Nuclear Is Now

I want to conclude by emphasizing that nuclear energy—combined with the use of renewable energy sources like wind, geothermal, and hydro—remains the only practical, safe, and environmentally friendly means of reducing greenhouse gas emissions and addressing energy security.

If the U.S. is to meet its ever-increasing demands for energy, while reducing the threat of climate change and reliance on overseas oil, then the American nuclear industry must be revitalized and permitted to grow.

The time for common sense and scientifically sound leadership on the nuclear energy issue is now.

Advances in Hydropower Technology Can Protect the Environment

Jill Davis

Jill Davis has written for Popular Science, Popular Mechanics, *and other publications. She is the former managing editor of* OnEarth, *a publication of the Natural Resources Defense Council, an environmental advocacy organization.*

It seems impossible that anything of technological significance could emerge from the basement of Richards Hall, the engineering building of Northeastern University in Boston. It is a haphazard warren, home to discarded office chairs, old lockers, and unclaimed pencils, all covered in a coat of fine gray dust. But it is also the home of the Hydro-Pneumatic Power Laboratory, where a 73-year-old Russian-born mechanical engineering professor named Alexander Gorlov spent a decade redesigning one of the world's oldest and simplest machines, the turbine.

Remove dams from the equation and electricity can be generated almost anywhere water flows.

Smiling, Gorlov walks over to a cluttered corner of the lab and wheels out a gurney. Strapped to it is an object that looks remarkably like an oversize beater from an old hand-held mixer. Still, this is it, the Gorlov Helical Turbine, which may someday help turn hydroelectric power into one of the most important and environmentally benign renewable energy sources on the planet. Gorlov's turbine received the 2001 Thomas A. Edison Patent Award, given each year by the American Society of Mechanical Engineers, which hailed its potential "to alleviate the world-wide crisis in energy."

A New Kind of Hydropower

The first thing to understand is that this is not hydropower as we know it. Just as wind turbines harness the kinetic energy of moving air, Gorlov's turbine has been designed to harness the kinetic energy of moving water—even slow-moving currents—without the need for dams. Remove dams from the equation and electricity can be generated almost anywhere water flows—in man-made canals, tidal straits, the open ocean, and unimpounded rivers. "Ocean and river currents contain a huge amount of energy," Gorlov says. "The question has always been: How can we get it without destroying the environment?" He is convinced that his turbine provides the answer.

This innovative form of hydropower is so new that its pioneers haven't even settled on a name for it. Some call it free-flow hydropower; others kinetic, low-head, or simply unconventional hydropower. Gorlov's design is one of many jostling for attention and investors. Companies in the United States, the United Kingdom, Norway, and Canada are building and testing their own free-flow turbines, but while the engineering can vary wildly, developers agree that free-flow hydropower has enormous potential.

One early prototype [of the turbine] . . . was used to recharge batteries at a village in the Brazilian Amazon.

The amount of power that could be produced from ocean currents almost defies comprehension. The currents flowing through San Francisco's Golden Gate alone, for instance, could produce an estimated 2 gigawatts per day—more than twice what the city needs at times of peak demand. The global potential is some 3,000 gigawatts, according to the United

Kingdom's Department of Trade and Industry. The agency estimates that 3 percent of that total, or 90 gigawatts, is economically recoverable using current technologies. . . .

Putting It to Work

In 1995, the National Institute of Standards and Technology's Office of Technology Innovation recommended that the Department of Energy consider supporting Gorlov's work. But that support did not materialize. Two years later, Gorlov conducted the first real-world test of his turbine in the Cape Cod Canal, where he experimented with models with two blades and three and with varying amounts of twist, looking for the design that would spin most efficiently in the current. Since then, in one pilot project after another, Gorlov has sought to prove to the world that his machine is commercially viable. The first projects were on a tiny scale. One early prototype powered a generator at the Tidewater Motel on the island of Vinalhaven, Maine; another was used to recharge batteries at a village in the Brazilian Amazon. Last summer [2004], a turbine was lowered from a barge into the tides near Shelter Island, in Long Island Sound. The most substantial feasibility project in the United States, supported by a $500,000 grant from the Massachusetts Renewable Energy Trust Fund, was a three-month trial near Amesbury, Massachusetts, in which four Gorlov Helical Turbines were submerged in the Merrimack River.

Considering the limited scale of these projects, Gorlov can count himself lucky that the Republic of Korea is facing an energy crisis. In 1999, an article on his turbine appeared in the *Financial Times,* and South Korea's National Assembly invited him to deliver a presentation on his invention. There were good reasons for the interest: South Korea's energy demands are growing at about 4 percent each year, and aside from a single natural gas field and some reserves of very low-grade coal, the country has no fossil fuels. To meet the burgeoning need for electricity, it relies heavily on imports and is planning to build several more nuclear power plants in the next decade. (It already has 19.)

However, the Korea Peninsula also happens to be home to some very fast-moving water. Soon after Gorlov's speech, the government pledged 40 billion won ($34 million) to develop a free-flow hydropower project driven by the Gorlov Helical Turbine.

A Test in Korea

On March 19, 2002, the Korean Ocean Research and Development Institute lowered the first Gorlov turbine into the Uldolmok Strait, a tidal channel that runs between the western coast of the Korea Peninsula and Jindo Island. The strait is famous for its roiling tidal currents, which can rip through the corridor at 12 knots [13.8 miles per hour]. Gorlov showed me a low-resolution video of the event on his laptop computer. During a lull in the current, workers struggle to get the turbine in the water before the tides come in. Just as it is secured, the murky brown water begins to surge and the blades start to move. Soon they are spinning wildly, cutting up the water, sending frothy chop into the air. Offscreen, workers shout with excitement.

Four months later, the institute hooked up the turbine to a generator. A second video shows the turbine spinning in the night. A light shines over it, using electricity produced by the tides of the Uldolmok Strait. It's hard not to compare the event with one that took place in Appleton, Wisconsin, in 1882. On September 30 of that year, H. F. Rogers, a paper magnate and Edison supporter who had built the world's first commercial hydroelectric plant dam on the Fox River, used his Vulcan Street plant to produce enough electricity to light a single house. It was reported that "men jumped up and down and screamed like school boys."

Last fall [2004], South Korea commenced the second phase of the project, when it installed a 15-foot turbine in the strait. During this phase, it hopes to produce up to 1,000 kilowatts of power that will be sent to Jindo Island, with a population of some 40,000. If that goes well, the government plans to install thousands of Gorlov's underwater turbines, hoping they can harness from Uldolmok and the surrounding oceanic streams up to 3,600 megawatts of power—about equal to the output of four nuclear power plants.

The Gulf Stream contains enough energy for all of North America.

Weighing the Pros and Cons

The success of the Korean project may largely determine the commercial future of the Gorlov Helical Turbine. Experts point out that the underwater environment is harsh and unpredictable, full of sediment, corrosive agents, and unforeseen events. "How long will the equipment hold up?" asks Joseph Sayer, a project manager at the New York State Energy Research and Development Association. "What happens if there's a storm? What about a log?" And of course each body of water is unique.

Yet another issue must be addressed if environmentalists are to embrace Gorlov's turbine. Richard Roos-Collins, a senior attorney with the Natural Heritage Institute in San Francisco and an enthusiastic backer of hydrokinetic technology, acknowledges that "if it turns fish into sushi, then it's got the same problem as wind power." (For example, the windmills at California's Altamont Pass Wind Resource Area kill up to 1,300 birds of prey a year.) Gorlov insists his turbines will create a pressure barrier that will keep fish away from the blades, but he has yet to prove it. Two summers ago [in 2003], Verdant Power placed monitoring devices on a single turbine and saw fish swimming around it. But what happens if fish encounter a whole field of whirling turbines?

None of these questions has stopped Gorlov from envisioning a world spinning with helical turbines, and that is a good thing. He imagines thousands of his turbines anchored near remote waterside villages, providing electricity to areas where there is no grid. He imagines pods of them linked together in streams and rivers. Most ambitiously, he imagines floating power farms that would harness the kinetic energy of the world's major ocean currents. "The Gulf Stream contains enough energy for all of North America," he says. Imagine a block of 656 Gorlov Helical Turbines anchored off the coast of Florida, where they could not only capture the enormous energy potential of the Gulf Stream, which carries some 80 million cubic meters [of water] past Miami's front door every day, but also produce hydrogen through the electrolysis of ocean water.

Concerns about money seem to irk Gorlov. "Perhaps it's reality that people first tend to compare the cost of installation and manufacturing, but think about it: We're not poisoning our air, our water, our environment." Who can argue with that?

Wind Farms Can Be Designed to Minimize Bird and Bat Kills

Hillary Watts

Hillary Watts is a contributing writer to High Country News, *a nonprofit newspaper covering communities and the environment in the American West.*

If you think wind energy is a good alternative to fossil fuels, but you also care about wildlife, you've probably worried about the possible "lawnmower" effect of spinning wind turbines on birds and bats.

At least some of that concern is justified. In the mid-1980s, people reported seeing piles of dead raptors at Altamont Pass Wind Resource Area near San Francisco, one of the nation's first wind farms. When a Sierra Club employee later described wind turbines as the "Cuisinarts of the sky," newspapers went wild with reports of hashed-up hawks, and opponents of alternative energy seized on this new excuse to halt wind-farm development. Another alarm was set off in 2003, when it came to light that turbines at the Mountaineer Wind Energy Center in West Virginia had killed about 2,000 bats in a two-month period.

Wind turbines do kill birds and bats, but the scale of damage varies widely, depending on several factors, including the wind farm's location, its turbine design, and the species of birds and bats that live nearby or migrate through. However, compared to the many other ways that humans kill winged animals, turbine blades generally cut only a sliver out of the pie.

The Extent of the Problem

According to the American Wind Energy Association, wind turbines account for only one out of every 5,000 to 10,000 human-caused bird kills nationwide. Many bird deaths are caused by communications towers, automobiles and domestic cats. The worst killers are glass windows: Researchers estimate that every year, 900 million birds die after slamming into these invisible barriers. But most of these victims are common city birds like pigeons and house sparrows.

Certain wind farms, like California's Altamont, do pose a significant threat to raptors. Altamont, a cluster of wind projects begun in 1981, was built "in the absolute worst place to put a wind farm," says Jeff Miller, a spokesman for the Center for Biological Diversity. The Center is suing Altamont to force it to replace many of its older, less-efficient turbines with fewer and taller powerhouses; this would reduce the blade gantlet, Miller says, and at the same time increase energy production.

But Laurie Jodziewicz, communications and policy specialist for the American Wind Energy Association, says Altamont is unique. Not only is the wind farm located in the middle of a major migration route, it has 7,000 turbines that spin at the same elevation at which hunting raptors normally soar. Modern wind farmers have learned from Altamont, and now try to build outside bird migration routes, minimizing habitat destruction by choosing areas that have already been altered by industry. And the new cylindrical towers are harder for birds to nest on than the old ladder-like structures.

The U.S. currently generates only about one-half of 1 percent of its energy from wind, according to Jodziewicz. Comparing the new wind technology to other sources of bird mortality—such as the Exxon Valdez oil spill in the 1990s, which killed an estimated 500,000 birds—she says, "Even if the U.S. got all its energy from wind, the percentage of birds killed by turbines would be small."

Bats and Wind Power

Merlin Tuttle, executive director of Bat Conservation International, says scientists know almost nothing about the relationship between bats and wind energy, except that the wind farms reporting high numbers of dead bats are located close to forested areas, which are used by certain migratory bats. Some researchers speculate that the bats' sonar may perceive the turbines' rotating blades as flying insects. But so far, he says, wind energy companies are reluctant to give bat biologists the permits they need to research turbine-related bat kills.

Until scientists do more research, new wind farms may not know how to be bat-friendly. Even so, Ed Arnett, a conservation scientist with Bat Conservation International, believes that "wind energy is a great thing," and notes that better siting and turbine design may solve the bat-blade dilemma.

Nuclear Power Threatens the Environment

Helen Caldicott

Helen Caldicott is a founder of Physicians for Social Responsibility, an organization of doctors opposed to nuclear weapons and nuclear power.

There is a huge propaganda push by the nuclear industry to justify nuclear power as a panacea for the reduction of global-warming gases. . . .

At present there are 442 nuclear reactors in operation around the world. If, as the nuclear industry suggests, nuclear power were to replace fossil fuels on a large scale, it would be necessary to build 2000 large, 1000-megawatt reactors. Considering that no new nuclear plant has been ordered in the United States since 1978, this proposal is less than practical. Furthermore, even if we decided today to replace all fossil-fuel-generated electricity with nuclear power, there would only be enough economically viable uranium to fuel the reactors for three to four years.

> *The nuclear fuel cycle utilises large quantities of fossil fuel at all of its stages.*

The true economies of the nuclear industry are never fully accounted for. The cost of uranium enrichment is subsidised by the U.S. government. The true cost of the industry's liability in the case of an accident in the United States is estimated to be $US560 billion, but the industry pays only $US9.1 billion—98 per cent of the insurance liability is covered by the U.S. federal government. The cost of decommissioning all the

Helen Caldicott, "Nuclear Power Is the Problem, Not a Solution," *The Australian*, April 13, 2005, p. 24. Copyright © 2005 The Australian. Reproduced by permission of the author.

existing U.S. nuclear reactors is estimated to be $US33 billion. These costs—plus the enormous expense involved in the storage of radioactive waste for a quarter of a million years—are not now included in the economic assessments of nuclear electricity.

Nuclear Power Contributes to Global Warming

It is said that nuclear power is emission-free. The truth is very different.

In the United States, where much of the world's uranium is enriched, the enrichment facility at Paducah, Kentucky, requires the electrical output of two 1000-megawatt coal-fired plants, which emit large quantities of carbon dioxide, the gas responsible for 50 per cent of global warming.

Also, this enrichment facility and another at Portsmouth, Ohio, release from leaky pipes 93 per cent of the chlorofluorocarbon [CFC] gas emitted yearly in the United States. The production and release of CFC gas is now banned internationally by the Montreal Protocol because it is the main culprit responsible for stratospheric ozone depletion. But CFC is also a global warmer, 10,000 to 20,000 times more potent than carbon dioxide.

Nuclear power is . . . not green and it is certainly not clean.

In fact, the nuclear fuel cycle utilises large quantities of fossil fuel at all of its stages—the mining and milling of uranium, the construction of the nuclear reactor and cooling towers, robotic decommissioning of the intensely radioactive reactor at the end of its 20- to 40-year operating lifetime, and transportation and long-term storage of massive quantities of radioactive waste.

In summary, nuclear power produces, according to a 2004 study by Jan Willem Storm van Leeuwen and Philip Smith, only three times fewer greenhouse gases than modern natural-gas power stations.

Dangerous By-Products

Contrary to the nuclear industry's propaganda, nuclear power is therefore not green and it is certainly not clean. Nuclear reactors consistently release millions of curies of radioactive isotopes into the air and water each year. These releases are unregulated because the nuclear industry considers these particular radioactive elements to be biologically inconsequential. This is not so.

These unregulated isotopes include the noble gases krypton, xenon and argon, which are fat-soluble and if inhaled by persons living near a nuclear reactor, are absorbed through the lungs, migrating to the fatty tissues of the body, including the abdominal fat pad and upper thighs, near the reproductive organs. These radioactive elements, which emit high-energy gamma radiation, can mutate the genes in the eggs and sperm and cause genetic disease.

Tritium, another biologically significant gas, is also routinely emitted from nuclear reactors. Tritium is composed of three atoms of hydrogen, which combine with oxygen, forming radioactive water, which is absorbed through the skin, lungs and digestive system. It is incorporated into the DNA molecule, where it is mutagenic [mutation causing].

The dire subject of massive quantities of radioactive waste accruing at the 442 nuclear reactors across the world is also rarely, if ever, addressed by the nuclear industry. Each typical 1000-megawatt nuclear reactor manufactures 33 tonnes of thermally hot, intensely radioactive waste per year.

The Nuclear Waste Problem

Already more than 80,000 tonnes of highly radioactive waste sits in cooling pools next to the 103 U.S. nuclear power plants, awaiting transportation to a storage facility yet to be found.

This dangerous material will be an attractive target for terrorist sabotage as it travels through 39 states on roads and railway lines for the next 25 years.

But the long-term storage of radioactive waste continues to pose a problem. The US Congress in 1987 chose Yucca Mountain in Nevada, 150km northwest of Las Vegas, as a repository for America's high-level waste. But Yucca Mountain has subsequently been found to be unsuitable for the long-term storage of high-level waste because it is a volcanic mountain made of permeable pumice stone, and it is transected by 32 earthquake faults. [In April 2005] a congressional committee discovered fabricated data about water infiltration and cask corrosion in Yucca Mountain that had been produced by personnel in the U.S. Geological Survey. These startling revelations, according to most experts, have almost disqualified Yucca Mountain as a waste repository, meaning that the United States now has nowhere to deposit its expanding nuclear waste inventory.

To make matters worse, a study released [in April 2005] by the National Academy of Sciences shows that the cooling pools at nuclear reactors, which store 10 to 30 times more radioactive material than that contained in the reactor core, are subject to catastrophic attacks by terrorists, which could unleash an inferno and release massive quantities of deadly radiation—significantly worse than the radiation released by [the nuclear accident at] Chernobyl, according to some scientists.

This vulnerable high-level nuclear waste contained in the cooling pools at 103 nuclear power plants in the United States includes hundreds of radioactive elements that have different biological impacts in the human body, the most important being cancer and genetic diseases.

The incubation time for cancer is five to 50 years following exposure to radiation. It is important to note that children, old people and immuno-compromised individuals are many times more sensitive to the malignant effects of radiation than [are] other people.

Health Threats

I will describe four of the most dangerous elements made in nuclear power plants.

Iodine 131, which was released at the nuclear accidents at Sellafield in Britain, Chernobyl in Ukraine and Three Mile Island in the United States, is radioactive for only six weeks and it bio-concentrates in leafy vegetables and milk. When it enters the human body via the gut and the lung, it migrates to the thyroid gland in the neck, where it can later induce thyroid cancer. In Belarus more than 2000 children have had their thyroids removed for thyroid cancer, a situation never before recorded in pediatric literature.

Plutonium lasts for 500,000 years, living on to induce cancer and genetic diseases in future generations.

Strontium 90 lasts for 600 years. As a calcium analogue, it concentrates in cow and goat milk. It accumulates in the human breast during lactation, and in bone, where it can later induce breast cancer, bone cancer and leukemia.

Cesium 137, which also lasts for 600 years, concentrates in the food chain, particularly meat. On entering the human body, it locates in muscle, where it can induce a malignant muscle cancer called a sarcoma.

Plutonium 239, one of the most dangerous elements known to humans, is so toxic that one-millionth of a gram is carcinogenic. More than 200kg is made annually in each 1000-megawatt nuclear power plant. Plutonium is handled like iron in the body, and is therefore stored in the liver, where it causes liver cancer, and in the bone, where it can induce bone cancer and blood malignancies. On inhalation it causes lung cancer. It also crosses the placenta, where, like the drug thalidomide, it can cause severe congenital deformities. Plutonium has a predisposition for the testicle, where it can cause testicular cancer and induce genetic diseases in future generations. Plutonium lasts for 500,000 years, living on to induce cancer and genetic diseases in future generations of plants, animals and humans.

Plutonium is also the fuel for nuclear weapons—only 5kg is necessary to make a bomb and each reactor makes more than 200kg per year. Therefore any country with a nuclear power plant can theoretically manufacture 40 bombs a year.

Damming Rivers for Hydroelectric Power Harms the Environment

Tim Palmer

Tim Palmer is an advocate for river conservation and the author of more than a dozen books, including Lifelines: The Case for River Conservation, *from which this viewpoint is excerpted.*

Strange and delusive myths have surrounded our use of rivers ever since Alexander Mackenzie and Henry Hudson sought the Northwest Passage and explorers wandered the Great Basin deserts in the early 1800s looking for the River Bonaventura. This "River of the West" was said to link interior America with the Pacific, but it existed only on maps and in wishful minds. Myths about rivers continue to abound, the most troublesome being those with some basis in fact. . . .

The Myth of Hydropower

One of the greater myths is that rivers can generate clean and cheap electricity to fuel a growing population while avoiding environmental pitfalls. In fact, the energy is not cheap and clean but costly and damaging on a scale rarely recognized, and the amount of power to be gained by damming additional rivers is small.

Inundation of thousands of farms in the Appalachians, incessant erosion of beaches in the Grand Canyon, and the extinction of salmon runs in the Northwest and New England are only a few examples of the hidden costs of hydropower. Though massive new dams have been defeated, . . . there remain a multitude of smaller hydroelectric proposals in the United States and modern megaprojects in Canada.

Less than one-tenth of U.S. electricity comes from hydro-power, and while maximized hydro development in this country would not boost that figure substantially, the specter looms that new dams could block hundreds of rivers. As supplies of oil and natural gas dwindle, as we awaken to the reality of global warming and acid rain emanating from fossil fuel use, and as our foray into nuclear reactors fails ever more decisively, hydropower, by comparison, will be painted as a benign bargain. Yet the sacrifice of aquatic ecosystems for electricity is one of the most troubling prospects ever faced by people who value rivers as they are.

Hydropower is produced when the force of falling water turns the wheels of a turbine, making electricity. Some small hydropower projects don't require dams but simply divert a stream's flow through a pipe, which runs steeply downhill to turbines in a generating plant. But to avoid low wattage in dry seasons, power brokers build dams to store water. With schemes of great complexity, engineers have designed tunnels to divert one river into another, and whole series of reservoirs release runoff to networks of canals, penstocks, and turbines, the river having been pressed by pipefitters into an outsized schematic of plumbing.

Hydro projects can require large initial investments but yield exceptionally long service lives and low operating costs, which means low rates on consumers' monthly bills, all of this owing substantially to environmental losses not paid for by the customers.

[Hydroelectric] projects decimated resident fisheries by flooding habitat and blocking [fish] migration routes.

America's Lost Rivers

The most obvious environmental cost of hydroelectric dams is that the reservoirs flood portions of rivers, causing them and their landscapes to utterly disappear. Hundreds of projects decimate resident fisheries by flooding habitat and blocking [fish] migration routes. Back-to-back dams on the Susquehanna [River] in Maryland and Pennsylvania flooded a wealth of river-bottom life and wetlands where the largest source of water neared Chesapeake Bay. Choice valley lands of the Little Tennessee, held sacred by Cherokee Indians and productively used for 200 years by mountain farmers, were flooded as recently as 1979 by Tellico Dam, though it contributes only 23 megawatts of power—0.1 percent of the Tennessee Valley Authority's supply. The Skagit River once ran as one of the most spectacular wild rivers of America, bursting with runoff from the alpine heights of Washington's North Cascades and plunging through rocky canyons shadowed by ancient trees of enormous girth. Even to the Skagit's headwaters in British Columbia, Seattle City Light impounded the upper river behind Gorge, Diablo, and Ross dams. Half of Hells Canyon—the celebrated second-deepest canyon in our country—lies beneath water dammed for hydroelectricity, interring what senior boatman Martin Litton described as a whitewater journey comparable to the Grand Canyon itself.

In an additional agenda of river loss, hydro projects divert water so that it bypasses its channel altogether, creating the ecological absurdity of a river in a pipe. Presumably the water is only borrowed from the stream. But in fact the diversion leaves the intervening bed dry and as conducive to aquatic and riparian life as corrugated conduit. Rivers such as the Sierra Nevada's Yuba and South Fork of the Stanislaus host complex schemes of piping, ditching, and tunneling from one valley to another to maximize the vertical drop, or hydraulic head, in the process reducing the integrity of the river that is left behind.

Finally, the flow regimes below hydroelectric dams are often given as little concern as a bathtub drain. Power companies cut off flows entirely as they recharge reservoirs; then they release torrents that scour riverbeds for peaking power two hours each afternoon. The results are degraded riverbeds and bulk losses of habitat caused by dam-induced erosion.

Hydropower's History

No one has calculated the losses of rivers and river life to power dams already built, yet hydro projects have been a source of destruction to America's native landscape dating back to the nation's first power plant, which was located on the Fox River in Wisconsin and lit 250 light bulbs in 1882. One of the initial efforts at natural areas protection in the nation was at Niagara Falls, with establishment of a New York State Reservation in 1885, but limitations on power development at the site were not recognized until later. Many of New England's 11,000 dams remain relics of a hydropower era that ignored everything else that rivers were good for. Nine dams on the Tennessee and forty-two on its tributaries constitute the most completely dammed large river system in America and flooded 635,400 acres—much of it productive farmland. Hydro dams in the upper Midwest block the Manistee, Pine, Middle Branch of the Ontonagon, St. Croix, and Namekagon—all outstanding rivers in other respects.

Gross reductions in natural rivers occurred up through the 1960s, and serious losses owing to hydroelectric development continue. One of the few big water projects to be built since the 1970s, a complex of four dams and diversions on California's North Fork of the Stanislaus and its tributaries Beaver Creek and Highland Creek, erased the singular beauty of Gabbot Meadow and one of the oldest structural remains found by archaeologists in North America. During construction of a project planned to provide a scant 7.5 megawatts of power, a diversion from the Fall River, below Yellowstone National Park in eastern Idaho, eroded through an embankment in 1992. A roiling, uncontrolled avalanche of water, rocks, and mud resulted in one of the worst water-quality disasters in recent Idaho history, ruining twelve miles of the pristine river and dumping debris into the Henrys Fork of the Snake [River].

Projects can be engineered for minimal impact, but developers tend to resist compromises.

Future Threats

No one can stand at the base of a hydroelectric monolith and deny that some projects produce a lot of power. Capable of generating 3,492 megawatts, Grand Coulee Dam ranks as one of the largest single sources of electricity in the world. A typical large hydro dam might produce 200 megawatts. To many people, that amount of power may be worth the cost. And, stirring little complaint, some small hydroelectric generators are innocuous. Fewer than 3 percent of the large dams in America produce power, and at many of these sites the harm has already been done; adding generators may cause little further loss. Ninety-three percent of the licensed or authorized hydro developments in 1989 occurred at existing dam sites. But, unfortunately, many of the retrofits depended on drying up new sections of river; half of the proposals in New England involved diversions causing dryways, some of them as long as 1,000 feet. Many projects can be engineered for minimal impact, but developers tend to resist compromises that forgo kilowatts.

Most hydropower plans go unopposed. In the 1980s the Federal Energy Regulatory Commission (FERC), the licensing agency for nonfederal power dams, permitted about 200 new projects annually. Only a few of the approvals each year met with strong objections by a broad-based river conservation community. Among thousands of hydroelectric projects in the nation's history, several score have been subject to concerted opposition. Several dozen serious proposals have been stopped by conservationists, and several hundred vaguely feasible sites have been precluded by protection measures. But many threats to rivers continue.

Wind Power Causes Too Much Environmental Damage

Iain Murray

Iain Murray is a senior fellow at the Competitive Enterprise Institute, a nonprofit public policy organization dedicated to advancing the principles of free enterprise and limited government. He specializes in global climate change and environmental science.

Wind power may well be the least environmentally friendly idea ever proposed by environmentalists. That certainly seems to be the verdict of those who live near proposed and actual wind farm developments in both the US and [United Kingdom].

Conservationists as committed as Sen. Edward Kennedy . . . and British television personality Dr. David Bellamy have come out against proposed uses of the technology. As a result, a degree of civil war has broken out in the environmental movement, with accusations of "NIMBYism" (the acronym refers to an aversion to new infrastructure projects, standing for Not In My Back Yard) flying around. One might even say that the controversy is generating a great deal of hot air.

The Cape Cod Controversy

The arguments over the proposed Cape Cod Wind Farm are a case in point. The proposal to build the USA's first offshore commercial wind-powered electricity generator in the waters off Cape Cod is partly a response to Massachusetts' new law requiring about 100,000 homes to be powered by renewable energy sources by 2009. The farm would consist of 170 wind

Wind turbines in northern Palm Springs, California, February 2006. Copyright © 2006 Kelly A. Quin.

turbines, each about 40 stories tall and covering over 28 square miles of shallow water off Hyannis, MA, and Martha's Vineyard. The farm would generate 420 megawatts of power. Proponents claim that this would replace the equivalent of 500,000 tons of coal or 113 million gallons of oil each year.

Yet the proposed benefits are not enough for some influential environmentalists. Citing the lack of a "programmatic environmental impact statement" and the absence of suitable state and federal scrutiny, Sen. Kennedy called the arguments for the project "loud rhetoric," writing in the *Cape Cod Times*, where he said, "Far more is at stake in the decision than our back yards, and I make no apology for opposing this project now." Sen. Kennedy and other locals are joined by national conservation groups such as the Humane Society of the United States, the International Fund for Animal Welfare and the International Wildlife Coalition. They point out that large marine wind turbine projects "may fragment vital bird habitat and alter migratory pathways."

Other environmental groups dismiss these concerns. Gary Skulnick of Greenpeace told the *Cape Cod Times* that, "Wind turbines don't make a lot of noise; they don't spew toxic chemicals. If I lived in the area, I would feel great about being on the cutting edge of innovation in this area. . . .You have to think of the big picture. If we don't reduce global warming, then Nantucket and all the beautiful beaches are going to disappear."

Wind farms are killing far more birds than the public realizes.

Europe's Experience

Similar arguments are taking place in the United Kingdom although the issue is much further along as many wind farms have already been built. A long article in London's *Observer* on October 5 [2003] pointed out the many and varied objections locals and environmentalists are raising against the wind farms springing up around the country in an effort to meet the United Kingdom government's target of generating 10 percent of electricity from renewable sources by 2010.

Self-professed "left-wing environmentalist," Martin Wright, told the paper: "Since the Second World War, there's been a consensus that landscape matters. . . . That's broken down here. If people in London knew the place, they would be appalled. And yet we're portrayed as nuclear-loving nimbies in the press. . . . Wind turbines are a good idea in the right place. . . . But sticking hundreds of them on wild land is not a good idea. For a small, heavily populated country we have some stunning landscapes, but they're under threat of industrialization."

The article also points out the threat to local avian wildlife:

Research shows, however, that wind farms are killing far more birds than the public realizes. A five-year study in California revealed that the Altamont Pass wind farm kills an average of 40 to 60 golden eagles a year, along with "several hundred" hawks, falcons and other birds of prey. In Spain, a report commissioned by the regional government of Navarra concluded that 368 turbines at 10 sites had killed nearly 7,000 wild birds in a single year, including 409 vultures, 24 eagles, and 650 bats.

In Germany, studies show turbines have killed dozens of rare red kites. . . . Red kites are a conservation success story, brought back from the brink of extinction in this area [of the United Kingdom], but two were killed at this small site alone last summer [2003]. Other rare British birds are also under threat as the turbines proliferate. . . . A farm of 27 turbines, each 325 ft high, at Edinbane on [the isle of] Skye has planning consent, despite RSPB [Royal Society for the Protection of Birds] objections that the site was too close to sea eagles and several breeding pairs of golden eagles, as well as merlin and hen harriers. All four species have the highest possible legal protection.

Other Worries About Wind

Finally, as energy consultant and TV personalty Professor Ian Fells pointed out, "To meet the 2010 target, Britain will have to build 400 to 500 turbines each year. Each will be a 3MW [megawatt] machine, bigger than anything yet seen. I think they'll be doing well to get there by 2020," Fells says. "There's some wishful thinking in the latest White Paper. And wind power is not completely clean. You have to build huge concrete foundations and service roads and so on."

Fells' fellow TV star, David Bellamy, has gone further. The conservationist has already led a march against one proposed new development and told the *Manchester Evening News*, "Wind farms don't work—they ruin people's lives, destroy the countryside, and harm wildlife. It beggars belief that certain members of the Green movement have bought into it."

There are plenty of reasons people are proposing these new commercial ventures, however. One proposed wind farm in West Virginia, would cost $300,000,000 to build, but would recover those costs and then some through various tax shelters and subsidies equaling $325,434,600. In many cases, the profit from this government largesse exceeds the income generated from electricity sales. Wind farm owners enjoy windfall profits at taxpayer expense. Green is very attractive when there are greenbacks involved whatever the harm to local avian life.

CHAPTER 3

Are Alternative Energy Sources Economical?

Chapter Preface

Many economists contend that before nations can transition to alternative energy sources, such sources must be able to compete economically with fossil fuels. Clearly, if it costs twice as much to run a home on solar power as it does to power it from electricity produced from fossil fuels, most consumers would balk at changing to solar power. On a larger scale, economists warn that forcing the nation to pay more for alternative energy would raise the costs of doing business, possibly grinding the economy to a halt. Unfortunately, in the eyes of many analysts, alternatives have not yet begun to compete satisfactorily with fossil fuels.

The case of hydroelectric power is an instructive example. On the plus side of the balance sheet, hydroelectric power seems to have many advantages over other energy sources. After the initial expense of building a dam, maintenance and operation costs are low. Moreover, unlike most other power sources, the fuel—water—does not need to be mined or processed, and it transports itself to the electrical plant, cutting out many of the costs associated with other energy sources. The secondary economic benefits associated with dams are just as important, according to supporters. These proponents point out that dams can create entire agricultural economies by making water available to otherwise arid regions. Indeed, dams often make it possible to farm previously unproductive areas. Dams also make rivers deeper and wider and thus navigable farther inland, easing transportation costs. In addition, dams produce enough cheap electricity to make energy-intensive industries like aluminum manufacturing possible.

Not everyone agrees that dams are beneficial, however. The economic benefits cited above often come at taxpayer expense, critics argue, because the federal government subsidizes the building and maintainance of dams. An economic analysis

by the Oregon Natural Resource Council, for example, concluded that dams on the Columbia River in America's Pacific
Northwest cost $87 million a year to run, much of which is
paid by taxpayers. Dams' impact on the environment also
carry an economic price, opponents say. Some fisheries experts blame dams in the Pacific Northwest for killing off much
of that region's salmon population, decimating a once lucra-
tive fishing industry. The federal government will spend $6
billion over the next ten years to modify eight federally owned
hydroelectric dams on the Snake and Columbia rivers to make
them less dangerous to salmon. According to the U.S. Fish and
Wildlife Service, these salmon restoration efforts accounted
for one of every four state and federal dollars spent on saving
endangered or threatened species in 2004.

The case of hydroelectric power illustrates that energy alternatives often come with a high price tag. Every energy
source has adverse economic impacts, but renewables—because they do not contain as much energy as do fossil fuels—
often cost more. In the following chapter authors explore the
economic advantages and disadvantages of alternative energy
sources. While the cost of using alternative energy is not the
only factor to consider in framing energy policies—people
may advocate for their use because they are less harmful to
the environment, for example—obviously such considerations
must be taken into account in order to create a viable energy
plan.

Wind Power Can Benefit Farmers and Rural Communities

U.S. Government Accountability Office

The Government Accountability Office (GAO) is the investigative arm of Congress; it issues reports on the receipt and payment of public funds.

Wind power does not currently contribute significantly to total farm income in the 10 states with the highest installed wind power capacity, although some individual farmers and rural communities have benefited considerably from this energy source. However, wind projects located on farmland have increased some individual farmers' income significantly, according to our site visits and analysis. In addition, large wind power projects established in some of the poorest rural counties in the United States have generally benefited these counties through the tax revenues they produce and the employment opportunities they provide.

Wind Power Is a Boom for Farmers

In the 10 states we examined, total net farm income exceeded $14 billion in 2002, but total direct income to all U.S. farmers from wind power ranged from only $10 million to $45 million, representing only a fraction of 1 percent of net farm income in these states. Nevertheless, wind projects located on privately owned farmland—the majority of U.S. wind power projects, according to AWEA [American Wind Energy Association]—have increased individual farmers' income by as much as tens of thousand of dollars annually, according to our analysis and site visits. In most cases, the farmers do not

U.S. Government Accountability Office, "Wind Power's Contribution to Electric Power Generation and Impact on Farms and Rural Communities," Report GAO-04-756 Renewable Energy, September 2004, pp. 34–38.

have an ownership interest in the projects. Rather, they receive lease payments from energy development companies for the use of the land and the associated "wind rights." According to AWEA and other sources, the compensation a farmer receives for leasing land for wind power turbines effectively amounts to between $2,000 and $5,000 per year per MW [megawatts of electricity] of installed capacity. However, actual compensation received varies widely, depending on the following factors:

- *The number of turbines.* One California project includes turbines with a total generating capacity of approximately 60 MW. Based on data developed from our site visit to this project, we estimate that one of the landowners has enough turbines on his land to have generated over $200,000 in annual lease payments from the project owner. In another case, an Iowa project consisting of about 260 turbines has a total generating capacity of approximately 190 MW. However, the turbines are spread out over separate properties owned by 65 farmers. According to the project owner and one of these farmers, the average annual lease payment is about $2,000 per turbine, with each farmer's total payments depending on the number of turbines located on that farmer's land.

- *The value of electric power generated by the project.* Land lease income is often linked to wind power project revenues. For example, land lease income may be a percentage of the gross revenues from the sale of the project's wind power. Thus, the higher the sale price of power, the higher the lease income to the landowner. The price paid by utilities for the electricity produced from wind power projects has varied by location and over time. Nationwide, these prices currently range from $20 to $35 per MW hours (MWh). However, power purchase contracts signed in California in the early 1990s tended to be well above this range. For example, the price currently received for electricity from one California wind power project is about $70 per MWh.

- *The terms of the lease payments.* The lease payments may include a single lump sum payment, fixed annual fees per turbine or per unit of power generation capacity, or a percentage of the project's gross revenues. The farmer may receive additional lease payments for other structures or considerations related to the wind project, such as substations, operations and maintenance buildings, and rights-of-way, including roads leading to and from the project and transmission poles and lines to connect the project to the local power grid. In cases in which the farmer has an ownership interest in the project, the potential financial benefits may be even greater per turbine. However, farmer-owned wind projects tend to be smaller, because farmers generally do not have the financial resources of an energy development company to establish larger projects with more turbines.

Additional income from the wind project helps keep the farm solvent and the farmer's family on the farm.

Wind Stabilizes Farm Income

Whatever the lease arrangements, the income farmers receive from wind projects located on their land is relatively stable compared with the income they derive from crop and livestock production, according to some farmers and other sources. Although the income from wind projects may be modest, these individuals said, it serves as an important hedge against possible fluctuations in income from crop and livestock production. Furthermore, income from wind turbines located on a farmer's land generally does not fluctuate significantly, although higher or lower average wind speeds from one year to another can affect the amount of royalty payments a farmer receives. Royalty payment rates—for example, 4 percent of gross revenues for electric power generated—are generally negotiated for a period of years. In addition, contracts between a landowner and a wind project owner often have a provision for minimum payment per turbine per year to protect a landowner's income in cases of unusual low-wind periods or if a turbine is out of operation because of weather-related damage or maintenance. In some cases, a farmer said the additional income from the wind project helps keep the farm solvent and the farmer's family on the farm.

Boosting Rural Economies

The construction and operation of a large wind project in a rural county is likely to increase the county's general level of economic activity and wealth. Constructing a large wind power project with several dozen turbines requires the services of multiple businesses and scores of skilled and unskilled workers, as well as the purchase of equipment and material, such as turbines, towers, asphalt, cement, concrete, and electrical cables. In these activities, wind power project developers and operators have directly benefited rural communities by hiring local people and purchasing locally some of the goods and services needed to construct and operate a project. Furthermore, according to DOE [the U.S. Department of Energy], increasing the proportion of the nation's energy generation attributable to wind power to 5 percent by 2020 would add about $60 billion in capital investment in rural America; provide an estimated $1.2 billion in new income to farmers, Native Americans, and rural landowners; and create approximately 80,000 new jobs. (To determine the overall economic benefits of increasing wind power to farms and rural communities, any losses to the fossil fuel industry need to be counted as an offsetting factor.)

In general, a county with a larger, more diversified economic base can more likely provide these services and supplies, thereby retaining more of the project's direct economic benefits. For example, according to the developers of a large wind project—High Winds in Solano County, California— they obtained much of the services and supplies needed to construct this project within the county, which has over 400,000 residents and a diversified business community. However, if a county cannot provide some of the services and supplies needed, other nearby counties or cities that can provide these services and supplies may benefit. In Pipestone County, Minnesota, for example, wind power developers purchased some supplies locally, such as concrete, but had to contract with a firm in Fargo, North Dakota, for a crane large enough to erect the turbines and with a firm in Minneapolis to do the electrical wiring. Pipestone County, located in southwestern Minnesota, has about 9,800 residents and a small business community.

> Businesses and individuals directly employed by the wind project are likely to spend part of their income at local businesses.

Indirect Benefits

Furthermore, businesses and individuals directly employed by the wind project are likely to spend part of their income at local businesses, such as restaurants, hotels, and gas stations, and hardware, clothing, and food stores. In some cases, the benefits from these activities may exceed the level of a project's direct benefits. For example, according to the Fort Stockton Economic Development Corporation in Pecos County, Texas, the county experienced a 10 percent increase in gross sales during the construction of several wind power projects.

The property tax revenues resulting from the establishment of a wind power project in a county creates additional revenues that support schools, hospitals, fire protection, and other public services. Following are some examples:

- Lincoln County, Minnesota, with a population of about 6,200, obtained about $470,000, or 18 percent of its property tax revenues, in 2003 from local wind power projects with a combined capacity of 156 MW.

- Pipestone County, Minnesota, obtained about $660,000, or 8 percent of its property tax revenues, in 2001 from wind projects with a combined capacity of 113 MW.

- In Pecos County, Texas, with a population of about 16,000 the school districts received about $5 million in 2002 from property tax revenues directly associated with wind power projects in that county. For example, the Iraan-Sheffield School District, obtained one-third of its property tax revenues from wind power projects that year. These projects also added about 30 to 35 full-time permanent jobs to operate and maintain the projects.

For some counties, tax benefits may have to be deferred to attract wind power developers. These counties have offered generous tax abatements, forgoing part or much of the tax revenues that would have otherwise been collected for the period covered by the abatement. For example, to attract wind power developers, Texas's Upton County offers a tax abatement of 10 years, waiving all property taxes during this period with the exception of taxes collected for schools.

In terms of other taxes, counties that have sales taxes or that receive a share of state sales tax revenues are likely to realize income from the sale of taxable goods and services connected with the construction and operation of a wind power project. In addition, in states that have a personal or corporate income tax, the increased employment and business opportunities associated with a wind power project are likely to increase these tax revenues, which are then shared with counties in the state or used for public projects that benefit county residents.

Rising County Employment and Income

To better gauge the significance of general increases in economic activity, we asked NREL [the National Renewable Energy Laboratory] to use its Wind Impact Model to estimate these benefits, as well as direct benefits, for the counties we visited. NREL developed a number of estimates, varying the size of the wind project but otherwise keeping key model assumptions constant. In general, the results of NREL's analysis confirm our observations from our site visits. For example, NREL estimates that the operation of a 150 MW project located in Alameda County, California—a county with a large population and diversified economic base—would result in the creation of 65 new jobs in the county and increase total income in the county by $5.4 million. However, the same size project located in Upton County, Texas, which has a much smaller population and economic base, would result in only 47 new jobs and an increase in total county income of $2.75 million. This is because in the case of Upton County, more of the staff needed to operate the project would be hired from outside the county. Nevertheless, the impact of the local hires on employment in Upton County may be greater than in Alameda County because the population of Upton County is so much smaller.

Solar Power Is Becoming More Economical

Nancy Stauffer

Nancy Stauffer is a writer and editor for the Laboratory for Energy and the Environment at the Massachusetts Institute of Technology.

Based on more than 200 interviews and detailed financial analyses of 150 solar power companies, an MIT [Massachusetts Institute of Technology] analyst has concluded that the tendency of energy experts and decision makers to dismiss solar power as "too expensive to be important" may be a big mistake.

Indeed, based on his findings, MIT graduate student Michael G. Rogol predicts that in 2015 solar power will make up a significant fraction of the new electricity-generating capacity added worldwide. And most of the additions will not be stand-alone systems in remote areas but rather grid-connected systems on people's roofs.

Throughout the 1990s, Mr. Rogol worked as a management consultant and market analyst focusing on oil, natural gas, and electric power. Like others in the energy field, he knew well that solar power was not economically competitive in the electricity marketplace. So why did he see more and more people in Japan and Germany putting solar panels on their houses?

A comprehensive financial analysis . . . confirmed that . . . solar power is indeed spreading.

Nancy Stauffer, "Solar Power Thru 2015: Re-evaluating Its Potential," *energy and environment*, March 2005. Reproduced by permission of *energy and environment*, the newsletter of the MIT Laboratory for Energy and the Environment.

Solar Power Economics

To find out, in 2003 Mr. Rogol began a two-year study of the solar power industry, through [MIT's] Laboratory for Energy and the Environment. He interviewed solar power executives, technologists, investors, and policy makers and performed a comprehensive financial analysis of the global solar power industry. His analysis confirmed that—despite the high cost—solar power is indeed spreading. "I found that the amount of new solar power installed each year [in megawatts] is 23 times greater now [in 2005] than it was in 1994," he said. "And almost everyone I've interviewed expects annual solar installation to grow an additional 20 to 25 times in the coming decade."

Three observations explain the apparent inconsistency between the high cost of solar on one hand and the fast growth in solar power installations on the other. First, when considering the economic viability of solar power, many energy analysts focus on the cost of generating electricity at large central power plants using traditional fuels such as coal, natural gas, and nuclear. That cost ranges from 2¢ to 8¢/kilowatt-hour (kWh)—far lower than the cost using solar photovoltaic (PV) systems, which ranges from 25¢ to 50¢/kWh.

Every time the manufacturing capacity for [solar] panels doubles, cost drops by 20%.

"But when residential customers think about installing a rooftop PV system, they compare the cost with the price they pay on their electricity bills," Mr. Rogol said. "And that price is much higher than the cost of generating the electricity at the central power plant." In some countries, residential prices are already high enough that solar power is almost cost competitive. A notable example is Japan, where residential customers now pay more than 25¢/kWh.

A second factor helping solar power overcome unattractive economics is the continuing drop in the cost of manufacturing PV panels and other PV system components. In the solar business, every time the manufacturing capacity for panels doubles, cost drops by 20%. Demand has grown by 35% a year for the past decade, so every two and a half years capacity has doubled. The result: annual cost reductions of 6–8%, which have largely been passed on to customers in the form of price reductions. . . .

Finally, most analysts do not recognize the magnitude of government support for solar power in many OECD [Organization for Economic Cooperation and Development] countries. In Germany, for example, if you put solar panels on your house, a government program requires your utility to pay you 70¢/kWh for your PV-generated power—well above the estimated 40–50¢/kWh cost of producing it. Indeed, if you take out a low-interest loan to install the panels, the check you receive each month is larger than the payment due on your loan. Other markets with strong policies supporting solar power include Japan, South Korea, Italy, Spain, China, and California and New Jersey.

Falling costs and strong government support have combined to make solar power economically competitive.

Rising Demand

Falling costs and strong government support have combined to make solar power economically competitive for many residential customers. As a result, demand has been growing quickly—so quickly that it has outstripped current supply. "Worldwide, the solar market is sold out through the end of [2005], and most capacity for 2006 has already been committed," said Mr. Rogol. "Ask your electrician to install panels, and you can expect to be on a long waiting list." To meet this strong demand, manufacturers are rapidly investing in production capacity, resulting in a projected sector-wide increase of at least 30% in 2005.

With so much demand from end customers, so much support from governments, and so much new manufacturing capacity coming online, Mr. Rogol feels confident that rapid growth in solar power use will continue. According to his estimates, in 2004 there was more than 1 GW [gigawatt] of new solar capacity installed worldwide—equivalent to adding one large power plant. By 2010 he estimates that the capacity added each year will be up to 5 GW and by 2015, close to 20 GW.

To put those numbers into context, the world's total electricity-generating capacity in 2004 was 3600 GW. Thus, the new solar capacity did not add significantly to total global capacity. But the story changes when we focus on annual additions to capacity. In 2004, new solar capacity accounted for only about 1% of total additions worldwide. "But given the rapid growth in new solar capacity, solar will likely make up some 5% of total annual capacity additions worldwide by 2010 and has realistic potential to be close to 20% by 2015," he said. "While solar will still be a small fraction of total global installed capacity, its importance in incremental capacity expansions will become much more significant."

The money involved is also significant. Revenue in the solar sector (including the prices paid for modules, inverters, other components, installation, and other fees) was about $7 billion in 2004 and should reach $10 billion in 2005—estimates based on Mr. Rogol's interviews with the largest solar companies. . . . Looking farther out, he predicts that by 2010 it is likely to rise to $30–40 billion, and by 2015 it might be as much as $80 billion. Why the dramatic growth? Not only are current companies expanding production but also new companies are joining the solar market, among them GE [General Electric] and others that have traditionally sold equipment for large fossil-fuel-fired plants.

Building with solar panels. Library of Congress.

Solar Power's Future

How confident is Mr. Rogol in his estimates? "I think through 2010 these are very safe numbers. I can see out to 2010 with my interviews and analyses because companies have already made commitments of capital and resources, and policies are already in place," he said. "Beyond that, corporate commitments and government policies become less certain." He emphasized that he is not alone in predicting rapid growth in solar capacity. Executives in companies such as Sharp, BP, Kyocera, Dow Corning, and Shell are now making major investment plans to expand their solar-related activities—strategic decisions consistent with expectations of continued growth.

All the good news for the coming decade is tempered by long-term challenges that may disrupt solar power's growth after 2015. As more and more people install solar capacity, government subsidies are likely to become prohibitively expensive and be trimmed back or eliminated sometime after 2010. And by about 2015, silicon crystalline technology will likely have reached maturity. While promising new manufacturing methods are delivering cost reductions, by 2015 all the potential benefits of efficiency gains, economies of scale, and so on will have been reaped. Further cost decreases will come only if new, more-efficient solar power technologies have been developed.

Therefore, timing is critical. If the present government subsidies for solar power continue until R&D [research and development] advances bring the cost of solar-generated electricity in line with residential electricity prices, then the role of solar PVs as a power-generation technology could become large. Noting that possibility, Mr. Rogol stressed the urgent need for "more work to be done to lay out a detailed, comprehensive analysis of the major challenges for solar power beyond 2015—challenges that we should begin to address now."

Geothermal Heat Pumps Save Consumers Money

Jessica Worden

Jessica Worden is a staff writer for E/The Environmental Magazine, *a journal of personal, community, and global environmental issues published by Earth Action Network.*

As the need for electricity continues to grow faster than the average American waistline, people like Philip Clark are moving beyond the fossil fuels that heat our homes, light our stoves and illuminate our streets. Instead, they're tapping into a natural source that is as old as the world itself—geothermal energy. "It's a common-sense approach to heating and cooling a building," says Clark, a Connecticut architect who installed a geothermal heat pump in his 5,200-square-foot, 300-year-old home.... Geothermal energy is a massive, under-exploited heat and power resource that is clean, reliable and local, he says. Clark sees the renovation of his home as an experiment to help save costs and the environment. "It does its job and it does it inexpensively," he says.

Hooray for Heat Pumps

A geothermal heat pump is an environmentally friendly device homeowners can use to siphon heat from the Earth's surface to use for heating, air conditioning and hot water. Unlike conventional furnaces that must burn fuel—usually natural gas, propane or oil—geothermal heat pumps simply take advantage of the Earth's natural heat. Typically, water is cycled through an underground pipe, and the heat in the surrounding soil warms or cools the heat pump's refrigerant. Hot and cool air is then distributed through a home by electrically

Jessica Worden, "Clean Heat: The Geothermal Energy Beneath Our Feet," *E/The Environmental Magazine*, January-February 2005. Reproduced with permission from *E/The Environmental Magazine*.

driven compressors and heat exchangers that employ the same principles as a refrigerator.

"It's a truly renewable system using heat from the Earth's surface and requiring a minimal amount of energy to deliver that heat," explains Lisa McArthur, a representative of the International Ground Source Heat Pump Association, a trade group. "The temperature underground is constant [low 40s in the northern U.S. to the low 70s in the South]. If a home needs to be heated in the winter or cooled in the summer, the energy source is in one's own backyard," she says.

McArthur, who has owned her own heat pump for about a year, says, "It's a quiet system and I am completely unaware it's there. The air quality is also better, and so are my allergies." Depending upon the size and quantity of heat pumps, a homeowner may expect to pay a few thousand dollars more for installation than for a conventional fossil-fuel system. But with geothermal, homeowners enjoy reduced energy bills, high reliability and long life.

Clark pays roughly $125 per month to heat or cool his 5,200 square feet. As for McArthur, her new 1,600-square-foot home is the same size as her old one but costs half as much to heat and cool. "It is constantly comfortable throughout, with no hot or cold spots," she adds.

According to the U.S. Department of Energy, geothermal technology can reduce energy costs 30 to 60 percent compared to traditional furnaces. This means a geothermal unit will pay for itself in two to 10 years. Subsidies and tax incentives, which vary from state to state, can make the systems even more affordable.

"There is always initial sticker shock, but our clientele is more concerned with the environment and long-term use rather than the initial bottom line," says Scott Jones, a sales manager at ECONAR, a Minnesota-based heat pump producer. According to Jones, experienced homeowners building or buying their third or fourth (and often last) home are often more open to considering the technology, since they know they are getting a long-term investment. "For every dollar put into the building and maintenance of heat pumps, there is $3.50 of output," adds Jones.

Former oilman President George W. Bush installed a geothermal heat pump at his Texas ranch.

Geothermal Goes Global

For many years, people in volcanically active places such as Iceland and New Zealand have taken advantage of the intense local geothermal heat to warm their homes and even produce electricity (by producing steam as water is pumped over the hot rocks). As a result, Iceland, for example, has largely been able to avoid the use of fossil fuels and boasts some of the purest air and water on Earth. However, the caveat of such renewable technology was always thought to be its limited geographic distribution.

But with advances in heat pump technology, geothermal energy is poised for widespread service beyond the denizens of Reykjavik [Iceland's capital city]. Experts say geothermal heat pumps can be used almost anywhere in the U.S. and the world.

Former oilman President George W. Bush installed a geothermal heat pump at his Texas ranch during the 2000 election campaign. The word in the industry is that Vice President Dick Cheney will soon be installing a heat pump at his private estate.

Large-scale geothermal power plants, which emit little carbon dioxide, no nitrogen oxides, and very low amounts of sulfur dioxide, are also feasible. The geothermal industry and the U.S. Department of Energy are developing technologies to recycle minerals contained in geothermal fluid so that little or no disposal or emissions occurs.

Supporters say that increased geothermal energy production could reduce dependence on foreign oil and help stem the flow of toxic emissions. One of our critical energy options, they say, may be just beneath our feet.

Wind Power
Is Not Economical

James M. Taylor

James M. Taylor is managing editor of Environment News, *a publication of the Heartland Institute, a nonprofit organization providing research and commentary on social issues.*

Wind farms proposed for the state of Kansas would take money out of citizens' pockets, harm the Kansas economy, and provide few if any environmental benefits, a new study finds.

The study, conducted by former New England Electric System Vice President Glenn Schleede and released on March 1, 2005, documents that Kansas consumers will pay higher taxes and higher electric bills if the state chooses to adopt wind power recommendations made by the Kansas Energy Council (KEC).

The KEC, in its *Kansas Energy Report 2005*, recommends Kansas bestow special privileges on the wind power industry, such as tax exemptions, direct cash subsidies, and a mandate that all Kansas citizens purchase a certain percentage of their power from large wind farms.

Flaws Noted in the KEC Report

The Schleede study, *Misplaced State Government Faith in "Wind Energy,"* begins with harsh criticism of the KEC, which was created by Executive Order in June 2004, for a lack of objectivity in its 2005 energy report.

According to Schleede, the KEC is not objective in its analysis because the group consists in large part of representatives of organizations that would benefit from an expansion of

James M. Taylor, "Wind Farms Costly for Kansans, New Study Finds," *Environment News*, May 1, 2005. Reproduced by permission.

wind power in the state. "The KEC may be somewhat unique since representatives of various special interests that would benefit from adoption of the KEC's recommendations apparently were permitted to be *members* of the Council" (emphasis in original).

By comparison, the Schleede study is self-funded, and Schleede has no financial stake in the outcome of the wind power debate.

Schleede writes, "the KEC has been misled by false and misleading information about wind energy" provided by the wind industry and pro-wind advocacy groups. "These organizations have consistently overstated the environmental and energy benefits of wind energy and understated the environmental, energy reliability, and economic costs."

Wind power is intermittent, unpredictable, and less frequent during times when electricity demand is strongest.

Wind Energy Potential Is Overstated

For example, the KEC asserts in its report, "Kansas' wind-energy potential ranks somewhere between first and third in the nation and is at least 10 times greater than the state's current electrical demand. . . . Should Kansas or any of the Plains states choose, electricity from wind power could become another exportable resource."

"These oft-cited claims are simply not true," responds Schleede. "They incorrectly assume that a *potential resource . . .* is an *actual, practicable, marketable resource* " (emphasis in original).

"Wind blowing over Kansas and the Great Plains is not a practicable, marketable resource for producing electricity," Schleede observes.

Schleede's study notes wind turbines can harness only a small portion of the wind; wind that is too light or too strong cannot be harnessed at all. Expensive transmission lines would despoil the landscape to bring wind from ideal locations to population centers. Finally, wind power is intermittent, unpredictable, and less frequent during times when electricity demand is strongest, such as during hot, humid summer days.

According to Schleede, approximately 21,000 giant wind turbines would have to be constructed and placed in the state to supply Kansas's energy needs under ideal conditions—which are, he points out, rare. More frequently, conventional power plants would still have to be running in backup mode to provide energy when wind conditions were not ideal.

Wind Power Is Prohibitively Expensive

Wind farms cannot displace conventional power plants; they merely supplement them, the Schleede study noted. Kansas consumers would be saddled with the costs of new wind farms and still pay for the conventional power plants needed to protect against blackouts when the wind doesn't blow.

"Wind turbines cannot be counted on to provide reliable generating capacity whenever customers need electricity," reports Schleede. "In fact, electricity consumers will, in effect, end up paying twice; first for the electricity from wind and then for the reliable generating capacity needed to meet peak electricity demand."

Tax avoidance and subsidy rather than meaningful power generation are frequently the primary motivation for building wind farms, notes Schleede. Tax breaks and subsidies are ultimately paid for by taxpayers and electricity consumers.

The wind industry receives a 1.8 cent federal subsidy for each kilowatt hour (kwh) of electricity it produces. The industry also is granted accelerated depreciation for federal tax purposes. Generous federal tax breaks for wind energy producers translate into substantial additional state tax breaks, because Kansas bases its state income determinations on federal calculations. Moreover, all wind power equipment has been granted full exemption from Kansas property taxes.

Even with generous subsidies and tax breaks, wind power remains more expensive to produce than coal, natural gas, and hydroelectric power.

"On December 15, 2004," notes Schleede, "an official from the firm of Milbank, Tweed, Hadley & McCloy, LLP, pointed out to the American Bar Association's Renewable Energy Committee that two-thirds of the value of a wind energy project comes from two federal tax breaks."

Also, Schleede observes, "A September 22, 2004, report by Citizens for Tax Justice claims that the FPL Group [a wind energy firm] paid no federal income tax in 2002 or 2003 despite having profits of $2.2 billion during those years."

Even with generous subsidies and tax breaks, wind power remains more expensive to produce than coal, natural gas, and hydroelectric power. As a result, wind power currently constitutes less than 1 percent of U.S. power generation.

Money Is Blowing Away

The wind power industry often counters these facts by asserting that expanding the state's use of wind power will create new jobs and economic benefits. Those claims, the Schleede study demonstrates, are misleading.

During construction of wind power facilities, a limited number of temporary jobs are created. Most such jobs last no more than six months, and they are typically given to workers with special skills, often imported from other states. Far fewer permanent jobs are created, and many of these, too, go to workers imported from other states.

Weighing against these relatively few jobs is the income forfeited by Kansans to pay for the substantially higher-priced electricity. Such forfeited income lowers living standards and silently eliminates a great number of jobs that a higher living standard would create. Worse yet, Schleede's report notes, most of the income paid for the higher-priced electricity would go to companies based in other states, further exacerbating the flight of dollars from Kansas.

Wind Turbines Harm Wildlife

Against all this economic cost, wind power might still be desirable if it provided substantial environmental benefits. Although touted as a "green" alternative to conventional power plants, wind power merely supplements them, displacing very little conventional power plant pollution.

But wind power imposes its own unique price on the environment. Wind turbines already in place across the U.S. directly kill hundreds of thousands of bats and birds (including endangered species) each year. The turbines disrupt aviary migration patterns and despoil landscapes.

Worldwide, Schleede notes, citizen environmental groups have risen up in opposition to wind power wherever turbines have been constructed or proposed.

"Other actions, such as using more energy efficient light bulbs, are much more cost-effective and environmentally meaningful," he concludes.

Solar Power Is Expensive

Kelly Spors

Kelly Spors is a staff reporter for the Wall Street Journal.

New federal tax incentives, along with soaring home-energy bills, might seem to brighten prospects for using solar power in the home. But environmental benefits aside, the economics of solar in many parts of the U.S. are still pretty dreary.

Even Tax Credits Are Not Enough

For tax years 2006 and 2007, homeowners can get a federal tax credit equal to 30% of the cost of buying and installing solar photovoltaic paneling or a solar thermal water heater, up to $2,000 per upgrade.

But that $2,000 tax savings won't shave much off the sky-high price tag of installing solar panels. A system of photovoltaic panels that convert solar radiation into a home's electricity often costs about $8,000 per kilowatt before incentives. That's a total investment of anywhere from $16,000 to $64,000, considering that most homes need between a two- and an eight-kilowatt system to replace most or all of their electricity needs. (The higher end of the range may include homes that use electricity to power their heating systems.)

Even with the new federal credit, it often takes 20 or more years to recoup the initial investment through energy-bill savings.

The credit makes a bigger dent for people buying a solar thermal water heater, which uses a special solar panel to heat a home's water supply. These usually cost about $7,000, so the $2,000 credit shaves about 30% off the price. (The federal tax credit can't be used if the solar water heater is primarily being used to heat a swimming pool or hot tub.)

Why Solar Is Expensive

Here are other considerations that determine the cost effectiveness of solar energy.

Solar panels need direct exposure to sunlight during the sunniest hours of day to generate the most electricity.

Ideally, the panels are placed on a large swath of roof that faces south or southwest and isn't obstructed by trees or buildings. "Shading is going to reduce your energy [production] quite a bit," says David Hochschild, executive director of PV Now, a consortium of solar-panel manufacturers. A south-facing roof gets 12% more solar radiation on average than one facing north, he adds.

Climate also makes a difference. Sunny regions like the southwestern states and Florida will provide more solar radiation than cloudier ones such as the Pacific Northwest. A photovoltaic system in Seattle, for instance, gets about 40% less solar radiation than one in Los Angeles, and Portland, Maine, gets 20% less than Los Angeles, according to the Solar Energy Industries Association.

It's mostly sun, not temperature, that determines the effectiveness of solar paneling. But snow that piles on a roof in winter can block the panels.

State Support for Solar

Several states have tax incentives that make solar systems far more economical. "It's really the states that are driving demand for solar, based on their incentives," says Ryan Wiser, a researcher at the Lawrence Berkeley National Laboratory in Berkeley, Calif.

Even with the best state incentives it still often takes more than a decade to recoup the cost of photovoltaics, although solar water heaters can often recover their investment costs in under a decade.

California provides an upfront incentive of $2.80 per installed watt—that is, $2,800 per kilowatt—for photovoltaic systems under 30 kilowatts. That's about 35% of the overall cost. California accounts for 85% of the solar-gear market in the U.S. In New Jersey, the rebate is an even greater $4.95 to $5.20 per watt, or about a 60% savings.

Among other states, Maine offers up to a $7,000 rebate on residential photovoltaic-system installations and $1,250 on solar thermal water heaters that runs through [2006]. Minnesota offers a $2 per watt—or about 25%—rebate. Sometimes utility companies offer their own rebate programs.

Some states offer extra incentives such as renewable-energy credits or exempting photovoltaic systems from property or sales tax. On the flip side, solar customers may be hit with high fees for connecting to the local electric grid, so it's important to look into all the financial ramifications before buying.

For a complete list of state incentives, go to www.dsire-usa.org and click on your state on the map.

About three dozen states offer "net metering," meaning residential solar producers can channel the excess energy they generate during sunlight hours to the local utility company, offsetting the electric bills they usually run up at night and on cloudy days. States vary, though, in the rates that apply to net metering.

How long it takes to recoup the investment costs also depends on energy prices. Those who live in regions with surging energy prices, such as California and the Northeast, will garner savings faster than those in areas with lower utility rates.

Breaking even on solar power also depends on whether the solar gear increases the resale value of your home—a topic on which the evidence is still fairly limited.

To get an idea of how long it might take you to break even, check out "My Solar Estimator" at www.FindSolar.com

online. Homeowners can also usually get a free analysis done by a local installer, but be sure to double-check the assumptions used.

Nuclear Power Is More Costly than Other Energy Sources

Pietro S. Nivola

Pietro S. Nivola is vice president and director of Governance Studies at the Brookings Institution, an independent research and policy think tank.

On average today, the electricity produced by operational nuclear plants in the United States tends to be cost competitive with gas or coal-generated power after the plants have been paid for. Indeed, the efficiency of quite a few has been upgraded, making them attractive to buyers. Between 1998 and 2002, more than a dozen old plants were sold, some fetching impressive sums. Large energy companies like Entergy, Dominion Energy, and Exelon recently have made such acquisitions, in part as a hedge against increasingly unstable fuel prices for gas-fired generation, and perhaps also in anticipation of possible further environmental restrictions on coal-fired facilities. Even foreign investors have been eyeing U.S. nuclear units. The British firm Amergen purchased three between 1998 and 2000.

The commercial viability, of reactors that have not yet been built is a different matter—at least for now. A recent Massachusetts Institute of Technology (MIT) study offers probably the best current estimate of the aggregated cost of constructing, licensing, and running a newly commissioned light-water reactor, and how it compares to the coal or gas substitutes. At an average of 6.7 cents per kilowatt-hour, the "levelized" cost of the nuclear plant decidedly exceeds that of a pulverized-coal-fired plant (4.2 cents/kw-hr). Nor does the nuke compete with a combined-cycle natural gas–powered plant (CCGT), even assuming a high price for natural gas. Thus, if gas were priced at $6.72 per thousand cubic feet, the lifetime average for electricity from the CCGT still comes to 5.6 cents/kw-hr, which is less than the nuclear plant.

It is well known that new nuclear plants take exceptionally long to complete and, according to many analysts, cost more than they should to build safely. But, says the MIT report, even reducing completion time to just four or five years, and lowering construction costs by a quarter, would still not put the plants in contention with coal, and would just barely match the price performance of a CCGT using high-cost gas. Clearly, these figures do not augur much renewed interest in nuclear construction projects, at least for the foreseeable future.

Let us look more closely at the roots of the nuclear sector's predicament to date.

Enormous overhead, which accounts for two-thirds of the cost of nuclear-generated electricity . . . puts it at a marked disadvantage.

Capital Costs: Inflated by Regulation?

Twenty years ago [in the mid 1980s] the cost of building a nuclear power station in the United States averaged almost $3 billion (in 2002 dollars). Years of technological refinements and potential cost-saving measures since then have not succeeded in significantly lowering that price tag. The persistence of this enormous overhead, which accounts for two-thirds of the cost of nuclear-generated electricity, is what puts it at a marked disadvantage against power from combined-cycle gas turbines or coal-burning plants.

Why capital costs are so prohibitive is a question much debated. We know that cost overruns have to do with delays in the construction process. Before 1979, it took an average of seven years for plants to go on line. By 1990, the average lag from groundbreaking to operation had reached twelve years. The delays, in turn, have been widely attributed to a ratcheting up of regulatory requirements for health, safety, and environmental reasons following episodes such as the Three Mile Island (TMI) [nuclear power plant] accident in 1979. One estimate imputed to the post-TMI standards as much as 60 percent of capital costs for plants completed after 1979.

There is little doubt that regulatory strictures have slowed construction time and added to expenses. But whether those strictures have been overcautious—or, more precisely, out of line with consumer preferences and market demand—is not so clear. Nor, more basically, is it clear that government regulation stalled nuclear projects more than did other factors. Energy markets underwent a seismic shift after 1974. Earlier, electricity consumption had been increasing at nearly 7 percent annually. At that pace, electric utilities could count on a doubling of demand for baseload capacity every ten years. Following the [energy] crisis of 1974, the growth rate of consumption year-over-year settled to an average of around 3 percent. Perforce, in this new world of softer demand, most utilities began rethinking commitments to big and costly capacity additions. New orders for nuclear plants in particular started falling off sharply, and dozens of standing orders were cancelled, even before the Three Mile Island disaster.

There is no question that Three Mile Island marked a watershed. After it, orders for nuclear facilities ceased. Interestingly, however, the cessation occurred almost everywhere—throughout the United States but also in all but three other OECD [Organisation for Economic Co-operation and Development] countries, irrespective of national regulatory systems. Was the collective retreat from nuclear investment attributable to an international wave of public hysteria, and of government red tape? More plausibly, what happened was mostly the culminating consequence of negative market trends that had commenced earlier, and that now were accentuated by further loss of investor confidence and by heightened (and not wholly irrational) revealed preferences for supplemental safety measures.

Competition from Gas and Coal

When measured on a present-value basis, the capital-intensity of a nuclear plant means that two-thirds or more of its costs may be incurred up front, before it opens for business—and that is without factoring in interest payments accrued during the long construction ordeal. By contrast, only a quarter of the costs of the typical gas-powered electric plant are front-loaded. No wonder that the latter have supplied almost all of the total new capacity added in recent years. The invidious comparison is a little unfair; many of the gas plants tend to be built to carry peak- or intermediate-loads, not baseloads. In most of the country baseloads are handled predominantly by coal-fired generators. These are not cheap. Their capital costs per kilowatt hour are more than twice those of combined-cycle gas turbines. Yet coal has been a formidable rival to nuclear power. Even with the latest clean-air gadgetry, coal plants are not as expensive to build as nukes, and once built, are relatively economical to operate because the price of coal has dropped steadily over the past twenty years.

In time, coal's importance to U.S. electricity producers may decline amid mounting concerns about its pollutants. But its dominance is not about to end swiftly. Coal's share of U.S. electric generation has, if anything, increased over the past several decades, reaching 50 percent in 2002. For the most part, the edge over nuclear energy simply reflects market forces: a nation so richly endowed with this particular fossil fuel naturally puts it to extensive use. . . .

New Investment Is Currently Unlikely

Eccentric government policies, including environmental ones, have not been the overriding source of the nuclear industry's tribulations in the United States over the past thirty years. Policymakers in a number of other industrial countries have distanced themselves from the nuclear enterprise, sometimes much more conspicuously than here [in the United States].

Rather, quite apart from lingering reservations about safety and security, four fundamentals continue to dampen enthusiasm for a nuclear renaissance in the United States today. First, annual growth in demand for power never returned to pre-1974 heights. Second, gas-fired technology is comparatively quick and inexpensive to install. Third, there is little economic incentive to retire the nation's vast coal-burning infrastructure. And fourth, lest we forget, more than a hundred old atomic reactors are still on line.

These realities have contributed to a plush reserve margin (nearly 30 percent) in the U.S. electricity business, and to even larger surpluses in some regions (a huge reserve margin of more than 40 percent in the Southeast, for instance). That much slack will not persist in the years ahead, particularly as the national economy regains a robust rate of growth, but contrary to the claims of alarmists, neither is a genuine crunch imminent. In this setting, investors are unconvinced that basic capacity enlargement, at least on a grand scale, is urgent. And for none is prudence more warranted than for those pondering the future of nuclear power.

CHAPTER 4

Should Alternative
Fuels Be Pursued?

Chapter Preface

In August and September 2005, Hurricanes Katrina and Rita swept the Gulf Coast of the United States, the region where nearly half of America's gasoline is produced. The hurricanes shut down or seriously disrupted nearly a third of that area's energy production. The sudden reduction in gasoline and diesel supplies sent already high fuel prices soaring to record levels. In many places around the country, prices spiked to over three dollars a gallon.

The energy shock triggered by Katrina and Rita raised questions about the wisdom of fueling such a vital sector of the economy—transportation—almost solely with petroleum. Sixty-seven percent of U.S. petroleum consumption goes to transportation, fueling the cars, trucks, airplanes, and ships vital to keeping the economy running. Eighty percent of the growth in U.S. fuel use over the next twenty years is expected to occur in the transportation sector. Even if the world's supplies of oil are not running out, as many experts predict, can they meet the expected growth in demand?

Many analysts believe the answer is no. They contend that alternative fuels must be developed as quickly as possible to avoid serious disruption to the American economy if diminished petroleum supplies or rising demand drive up fuel prices. To the analysts' way of thinking, diversifying the kinds of fuel America uses for transportation would spread fuel production over a wider geographic area, leaving the fuel supply less vulnerable to natural disasters.

Not everyone agrees with this argument, however. Other experts assert that the best thing for the American economy is cheap fuel. At present, these observers point out, alternative fuels cost more than petroleum does. A switch to such fuels would raise the costs of doing business, thereby harming the economy. Rather than invest in alternative fuels, these experts contend, the United States should increase domestic oil production. Opening up public lands for energy development would increase supplies, thereby lowering prices. Moreover, spreading production over a larger geographic area would lower the possibility that a natural disaster in one region would lead to price spikes for the entire nation.

Hurricanes Katrina and Rita made clear how vulnerable America's transportation sector is to energy-supply disruptions. The authors in the following chapter investigate whether or not transitioning to alternative energy sources might help mitigate problems such as those caused by Katrina and Rita, as well as other problems associated with the nation's reliance on petroleum.

Hydrogen Fuel Can Power Cars

Paul Strand

Paul Strand is a senior correspondent in Washington for the Christian Broadcasting Network.

Conservatives and liberals seem more divided than ever these days. But there is one issue that has become so critical it is bringing some from even the far Right and far Left together—breaking America's addiction to foreign oil. A broad coalition is forming to take the country in a new way—the hydrogen highway.

America's Oil Addiction

There are some downsides to American drivers' gas-guzzling, do-your-own-thing way of life.

For instance, the jam-packed streets of New York, the clogged roads into Washington, D.C., and the maxed-out freeways of Los Angeles, all places where millions of drivers everyday are poisoning themselves and all those around them. And helping to keep America dangerously dependent on oil from often-hostile states.

The war on terror and [the terrorist attacks of] 9-11 [2001] have rammed home the reality that sheikhs and ayatollahs can now hold the oil-addicted West hostage because most of the world's oil is beneath their sands. And terrorists could attack oil facilities or pipelines over there almost anytime and send prices skyrocketing.

It used to be mostly the environmentalists who were anti-oil. But now that it is a vital national security matter, many more people, even among the oil companies and automakers, are saying that this oil-addiction must be broken.

General Motors spokesman Dave Barthmuss said, "We simply cannot rely on countries that simply don't like us for our fuel."

And Frank Gaffney, a defense hawk and as neo-con[servative] as they come, remarked, "For national security reasons, we've got to get off imported oil."

He added, "We are relying on nations to supply us oil who are unstable at best, and downright dangerous and hostile at worst. Many of them support terror with the proceeds of our oil revenues."

Gaffney and allies of his on both right and left are promoting hi-tech breakthroughs that now make possible fueling systems and homegrown fuels that could give our cars 500 miles to the gallon. Yes, 500.

Gaffney said, "These involve alcohol-based fuels like ethanol, not just from corn, but from other sources; and methanol, which can come from places like trash-dumps and coal."

There would be little foreign oil left in a tank of gas then.

The Hydrogen Solution

Others, President Bush and California Governor Arnold Schwarzenegger among them, are pushing for something even more radical: getting rid of the gas tank altogether and replacing it with hydrogen power.

Bush has already committed close to two billion dollars to jumpstart converting the country to hydrogen. And Schwarzenegger is pushing to get 200 hydrogen filling stations built [by 2010], part of an ambitious plan to build a "hydrogen highway" stretching from Vancouver, British Columbia, all the way down to Baja, California.

With Californians buying one-fifth of the country's cars, their going hydrogen in the next few years would be a huge leap forward in turning the whole nation away from oil.

They call this a "disruptive technology." Imagine the world of gasoline-powered cars completely thrown out and replaced with a hydrogen economy.

Barthmuss stated, "These hydrogen fuel-cell vehicles will do to today's cars and trucks what today's cars and trucks did to the horse and buggy of 150 years ago."

Hydrogen is the most abundant element in the universe. You can get it many ways—from water, by pulling the hydrogen (or H_2) out of the H_2O, using renewable resources like solar, geothermal, wind-power or something called biomass.

The only by-product [of hydrogen fuel-cell power] is water vapor.

Bill Reinert at Toyota explains that biomass is, ". . . crop waste. It's maybe the husks and hulls from the corn, or the stalks and stuff like that, and really a step toward compost."

Reinert explained the process: "Fuel cells in an H_2-powered car work pretty simply. All you're doing is combining hydrogen with oxygen—you get an electrical reaction—[and] produce electricity."

And that runs the vehicle. When you use gasoline in a car, the result is a lot of pollution. But when you use hydrogen, said Reinert, ". . . the only by-product is water vapor."

An End to Smog

So you could kiss much of that smog choking our cities good-bye. That is the dream of folks like Cynthia Verdugo-Peralta, who works in the Air Quality Management District that includes Los Angeles, usually the number one city for smog.

And almost all of it comes from vehicles.

Verdugo-Peralta said, "Primarily it's 88 percent mobile sources."

The manager of the lab that tracks L.A.'s smog showed us just how filthy it is. He gave us a sterile filter, and then showed us a map of just what happens to such lily-white filters when they are placed around the L.A. area for just 24 hours.

None come even close to meeting the state standard for clean air. Think of the day when H_2-power makes all that go away.

Terri Alpert is just your everyday entrepreneur who sells sophisticated kitchenware from a big warehouse in Connecticut. But she started up the Web site HydrogenHighway.com after getting all excited about how hydrogen could transform our world.

Alpert said, "You can't tell me that even if natural gas is the source of that hydrogen, that while you're sitting in that traffic in L.A. and the only thing you're breathing in is air and water vapor, that the quality of your life hasn't improved tremendously."

And she said, "As I started to think about the ripple effects, I just saw this enormous revolution in the making."

Like the fact you can get H_2 from so many sources.

'The beauty of hydrogen is that no one country or no one region of the world can own the energy source.'

No More Foreign Oil Dependence

Chris White works at the California Fuel Cell Partnership, where automakers, energy companies and government are all working together to create the hydrogen highway.

White said, "The beauty of hydrogen is that no one country or no one region of the world can own the energy source. It can be manufactured by every country, every region, in the way that makes the best sense for them."

Alpert agreed, saying, "Because you can get it from almost anything, you're not dependent on anyone."

White says that one reason power is so expensive is the cost of getting it, producing it, transporting it. But hydrogen could be home-made.

White said, "It is entirely possible that one day we could have refueling stations in-home, with a fuel-cell connected, [and] that fuel-cell could power our houses, and then at night while we're asleep, that power could be re-directed into creating hydrogen that we'd be storing [to] put in our vehicles."

But the dream is a ways off. Right now, it takes one or two million dollars to create these prototype hydrogen cars driving around California and a few other select locations.

So, furious experimentation will be going on to cut those costs drastically.

Reinert said, "Unless we got a lot of customers willing to pay a million dollars, and in that case . . . well, we're done. Give us a call."

In California, CBN [Christian Broadcasting Network] News had a chance to try out Toyota, Daimler-Chrysler and Honda hydrogen prototypes. Right now, you are probably not going to find one down at your Honda lot, because they cost in the seven figures to make. But the technology is coming along. One we tried drives real smooth, and is very quiet. It gets up to 93 miles per hour.

Another challenge is getting the range way up. Most of the models so far cannot go as far as 200 miles before needing to refuel.

'Hydrogen is as safe, if not safer than gasoline.'

But all the car companies think they can double that in the months ahead.

Then there is getting rid of the public's nagging perception that hydrogen is not quite safe.

Barthmuss scoffs at such a worry. "Nobody thinks twice about sitting on top of a 30-gallon gasoline tank in a vehicle right now—much more volatile, much more flammable than hydrogen. Hydrogen is as safe, if not safer than gasoline."

The Hydrogen Future Is Near

Energy Secretary Samuel Bodman predicts that consumers will be happily buying hydrogen-cars in large numbers by 2020 or so.

Bodman commented, "There's every reason to believe that we will be successful. Now there are a lot of technical problems that need to be overcome to get there. But I'm reasonably comfortable, based on what I now know."

President Bush has pushed the Energy Department to work together with inventors, teams of automakers and researchers from the energy companies.

And they are all pushing forward as fast as possible, to make affordable hydrogen vehicles and the infrastructure to support them a reality.

Verdugo-Peralta remarked, "We're all onboard on this, and going in the same direction, which is unique in itself."

Sure, the cars are going to be small at the start, and their range may not be that far. But with all sectors of the economy working together, imagine how quickly this technology can evolve in just the next five, 10, or 15 years.

Vegetable Oil Can Replace Diesel Fuel

Mary DeDanan

Mary DeDanan is a Northern California writer, poet, and photographer. She is also recipient of the Best of West By Northwest.org Award for outstanding contributions to electronic journalism and media.

Is it possible to save civilization with a barrel of leftover fry oil?

Jessy Pope is giving it a good try. On a warm Santa Rosa [California] morning, in a cavernous garage, she and a half-dozen guys hover over their respective car engines, intent on installing hoses, filters, fuel heaters and yet more hoses. "This is another step in making the things I use in my life sustainable," she says. Rusty Davis, the workshop facilitator, walks around with soft advice and a strong wrench, demystifying the details. His motivation: "I want people to know that there are alternatives that work, that they're not grounded into supporting war."

These people are converting their diesel engines to run on vegetable oil, thus posing the inevitable question: Does the progressive agenda smell like french fries?

Every time there's a spike in gas prices, the alternative looks more and more possible.

A Growing Movement

There's Jessy and her boyfriend Michael Schindler, a cute young couple with an older Mercedes wagon. She'll be driving it to ferry her young nature camp students around. Wine-maker George Davis, sweating a little under the hood of his VW Passat, runs his biodynamic Healdsburg vineyard entirely on veg oil. (But he had a head start, he's Rusty's dad.) The energetic guy from Pt. Reyes Station [California], James Stark, is a partner in the Permaculture Institute and secretly lusts for a veggie sports car. Owner of the garage, Donnovan Watt, has a hint of the Caribbean in his speech; he works with Alexander Noack, straight in from Germany. Kind, groovy folks, no doubt, but revolutionaries? Yes. By the end of the day, they will have kissed off big oil, rejected resource wars and taken a big step off the treadmill of planetary destruction. And they can still go to the drive-in on Saturday night.

Unless you live in a bomb shelter, you know the big picture. Start with global warming, fed by emissions of your car, my car, everyone's car. As a group, we slurp up the fossil fuels, even when we know our behavior will eventually cause climate chaos (even the Pentagon knows it). Then there's peak oil theory: Petroleum is finite, we're reaching the point when it's not going to be so easy to get out of the ground, thus price and availability are soon to be radically altered ... with one or two little consequences, like war and societal collapse. Yet it's easy to forget (or deny) all this when we need to get around. We're busy, dammit. What's an Earth-sensitive person, with appointments scattered over three counties, to do?

Originally all diesels were made to burn vegetable fuel.

Jessy, George and an estimated one thousand others like them (just in the local area) are able to drive guilt-free. Interestingly, the [San Francisco] Bay Area has the largest concentration of alternative-fueled vehicles in the country. And the numbers are growing. Every time there's a spike in gas prices, the alternative looks more and more possible.

The fact is, it's not that hard.

Vegetable Fuel Benefits

Dr. Rudolf Diesel first showcased his amazing new engine at the 1900 World Exhibition in Paris, running on peanut oil. Originally all diesels were made to burn vegetable fuel, and actually last longer when they do. After the inventor's death in 1913, his design was modified to run on that new-fangled petroleum fuel. Decades later, it's easy to modify it back to veg. You change bits of the fuel system, add a little heater to liquefy the grease, and change filters often. For most veg drivers, a bit of tinkering is the norm, although you don't need to be a mechanic. Straight veggie oil conversion, as it's called, or SVO, works best for people who make a little extra effort. If you're sloppy in the details or lazy in the maintenance, you'll have problems.

It's all fairly new in the U.S., since the late '90s, with vegmobiles showing up at eco fairs and touring the country, wowing the media as they go. What's particularly caught on here is recycling waste veg oil, the stuff left behind in the restaurant fry vat. Recycling adds a layer of satisfaction, knowing that you are reusing a waste product that would otherwise be dumped. Bear in mind, these drivers must be religious about filtering the fat. But they drive around for pennies, and leave a waft of fish and chips behind them, instead of "dino-diesel" stench.

It's also considerably cleaner than dino-diesel. No sulfur (major component in acid rain), no net carbon dioxide [CO_2] (plants that produce oil are also absorbing [CO_2] in roughly the same ratio), considerably less carbon monoxide, soot, hydrocarbons and so on. Biodiesel (processed biofuel) and SVO do emit nitrous oxide (laughing gas), an air pollutant, in about same amounts as fossil diesel. It may vary by individual engine, its age and fuel (soybean oil is worse than canola, for instance). At least one expert, Joshua Tickell, recommends adding a catalytic converter to lower N_2O.

A Proven Alternative

Alexander Noack, the German at the workshop, is a rep from Elsbett Technologie, a stalwart firm in the diesel business. He reports that Germans have been running their vehicles on veg oil for the past 30 years, since the '70s oil crisis. Few drivers there burn recycled oil because "there aren't many McDonald's." They prefer the virgin stuff. . . . "We don't just think about the environment, we think about fuel prices, too."

Regular diesel costs the equivalent of $4 a gallon in Europe; new canola oil is about 30 percent cheaper. It also benefits local farmers, who have a new market for oil crops. Noack estimates that 10,000 Germans now drive veg cars. The German government has encouraged the trend by declaring this fuel tax-free until 2008, and setting quality standards.

Modifying the engine to run on straight vegetable oil is one approach. It costs upfront. There is another way to drive nearly guilt-free, and that's to modify the fuel. Biodiesel (which you buy from a distributor) does precisely that. A simple comparison: Straight veg is for people who don't mind getting their hands greasy; biodiesel is for those who just want to put it in the car and go.

Refined Vegetable Oil Biodiesel

Also made from vegetable oil, biodiesel is chemically altered to replace its glycerin with methanol, resulting in lower (thinner) viscosity. It can be run as-is in an unmodified diesel engine—although there are tricks to making it work, especially if you've been burning dirty dino-diesel for years. It's not cheap, either, currently [September 2004] running about $3.50/gallon retail. It's possible to make your own home-brew biodiesel from waste veg oil, although opinions vary on overall feasibility. It's not for the timid—the process can be nasty and requires care. It helps if you liked to play with chemistry sets as a child.

Most biodiesel drivers opt for the commercial stuff, higher price or not. They're willing to pay more as a matter of ethics, voting with their dollars for a sustainable future. Full disclosure here: The author, yours truly, is an occasional driver of a biodiesel pickup. When behind the wheel, I could be cited for smugness.

The problems are finding the stuff and getting good quality. There are very few places where you can just pull in and fill up with biodiesel. There was one infamous try in Fairfax [California] recently, which closed after (according to those who used it) it sold poor quality fuel, and was deathly slow in paying its suppliers. A brand new pump is rumored to be opening in south Santa Rosa, but not even its parent company, San Francisco Petroleum, could tell me where, when or how. At this point, your best bet is to get the stuff delivered to your home (it's very safe to store), or join a co-op.

In Europe, where over 5 billion gallons of biodiesel are sold annually, standards are clear, facilities available and the price competitive with regular petrol. In the U.S., it's an infant industry, just finding its feet, and stumbling now and then. Biodiesel use in the U.S. has jumped from half-a-million gallons in 1999 to 25 million gallons in 2003. That's still a tiny percentage, but growing. Part of the push comes from new government requirements that public fleets run at least partially on alternative fuels. (Example: The garbage trucks of Windsor [California] now run on biodiesel.) There's also high interest in protecting schoolchildren from highly carcinogenic dino-diesel fumes spewed from their own school bus. Clearly, it's a growth market.

Ethanol Can Replace Gasoline

Nathan Glasgow and Lena Hansen

Nathan Glasgow and Lena Hansen are researchers at the Rocky Mountain Institute (RMI), a nonprofit alternative energy research and consulting organization.

Biofuels, and specifically ethanol, have been the subject of a great deal of criticism . . . by detractors claiming that more energy is required to produce ethanol than is available in the final product, that it is too expensive, and that it produces negligible carbon reductions. These critiques are simply not accurate. State-of-the-art technologies have been competently forecasted—even proven in the market—to produce ethanol that is far more cost-effective and less energy-intensive than gasoline. We'll explore why, and why the critics have gotten it wrong.

When we say *biofuels*, we mean liquid fuels made from biomass—chiefly biodiesel and ethanol, which can be substituted for diesel fuel or for gasoline, respectively. The technology used to produce biodiesel is well understood, although its biomass feedstocks are limited and production today is fairly expensive. We will instead focus on ethanol, which we believe has significantly greater potential.

Ethanol, which can be substituted for or blended with gasoline, has traditionally been produced from either corn or sugarcane feedstocks. In fact, Brazil currently meets more than 25 percent of its gasoline demand with ethanol made from sugarcane. (The sugar is so cheap that the resulting ethanol sells in New York for $1.10 a gallon—with about 81 percent the energy content of a gallon of gasoline—after paying a 100 percent duty, illegal under WTO [World Trade Organization] rules, to protect U.S. corn farmers. Undeterred, the Brazilians are merrily expanding their ethanol exports to Asia.) Even gasoline in the United States contains, on average, 2 percent ethanol. . . . American ethanol is almost exclusively made from the kernels of corn, accounting for about 7 percent of the corn crop. But conventional processes and feedstocks used to make ethanol are not feasible in the United States on a large scale for three reasons: they're not cost-competitive with long-run gasoline prices without subsidies, they compete with food crops for land, and they have only marginally positive energy balances.

Ethanol from Cellulose

Happily, in addition to starch-based feedstocks, ethanol can be produced from "cellulosic" feedstocks, including biomass wastes, fast-growing hays like switchgrass, and short-rotation woody crops like poplar. While not cost-competitive today, already observed advances in technology lead us to believe that in the next few years, ethanol made from these crops will become cost-competitive, won't compete with food for cropland, and will have a sizeable positive energy balance. Indeed, because these crops are expected to have big biomass yields (~10–15 dry tons/acre, up from the current ~5 dry tons/ acre), much less land will be required than conventionally thought. Further, cellulosic ethanol will typically have twice the ethanol yield of corn-based ethanol, at lower capital cost, with far better net energy yield.

A common complaint about ethanol is that the quantity of feedstocks is limited and land used to grow feedstocks could be put to better use. For cellulosic feedstocks, the situation is quite the contrary. Cellulosic feedstocks are plentiful: for example, municipal and agricultural wastes can be used to create ethanol, with the positive side-effect of reducing the quantity of waste we must dispose of. Using waste to produce fuel has the clear benefit of a virtually free feedstock, and because energy is generally expended to create the product, not the waste, this type of ethanol obviously has a positive energy balance.

Not quite as obvious is to what extent dedicated energy crops can be used to produce ethanol. We believe the answer is straightforward. Research by Oak Ridge National Laboratory shows that dedicated energy crops can be grown without competing with food crops because they can be grown in marginal areas unsuited for food crop production, or on about 17 million acres of Conservation Reserve Program land that is currently being withheld from agricultural use.

Cellulosic crops have additional environmental benefits for several reasons. First, because crops like switchgrass are deep-rooted perennials, growing them actually prevents soil erosion and restores degraded land. For this same reason, cellulosic crops also have significantly lower carbon emissions. While corn-based ethanol reduces carbon emissions by about 20 percent below gasoline, cellulosic ethanol is predicted to be carbon-neutral, or possibly even net-carbon-negative.

'Doesn't ethanol require more energy to produce than it contains?' The simple answer is no.

The Ethanol Energy Balance

We can't remember how many times we've been asked the question: "But doesn't ethanol require more energy to produce than it contains?" The simple answer is no—most scientific studies, especially those in recent years reflecting modern techniques, do not support this concern. These studies have shown that ethanol has a higher energy content than the fossil energy used in its production. Some studies that contend that ethanol is a net energy loser include (incorrectly) the energy of the sun used to grow a feedstock in ethanol's energy balance, which misses the fundamental point that the sun's energy is *free*. Furthermore, because crops like switchgrass are perennials, they are not replanted and cultivated every year, avoiding farm-equipment energy. Indeed, if poly-cultured to imitate the prairies where they grow naturally, they should require no fertilizer, irrigation, or pesticides either, So, according to the U.S. Department of Energy, for every one unit of energy available at the fuel pump, 1.23 units of fossil energy are used to produce gasoline, 0.74 of fossil energy are used to produce corn-based ethanol, and only 0.2 units of fossil energy are used to produce cellulosic ethanol.

Critics further discount cellulosic ethanol by ignoring the recent advancements of next-generation ethanol conversion technologies. A recent example that has received significant attention is David Pimentel's March 2005 paper in *Natural Resources Research* which argues that ethanol production from cellulosic feedstocks requires more fossil energy to produce than the energy contained in the final product. However, Pimentel bases his analysis on only one technology used to produce ethanol, ignoring two other developing technologies. His chosen conversion technology, acid hydrolysis, is the least efficient of the three.

Improving Ethanol Production

A superior option, thermal gasification, converts biomass into a synthesis gas composed of carbon oxides and hydrogen. The gas is then converted into ethanol via either a biological process using microorganisms or a catalytic reactor. Both of these processes show good potential for increased energy yields and reduced costs by using cellulosic feedstocks. This conversion technology is currently being tested in pilot plants in Arkansas and Colorado.

Still better, enzymatic reduction hydrolysis already shows promise in the marketplace. Such firms as Iogen and Novozymes have been developing enzymes, and "smart bugs," that can turn biomass such as corn residues (leaves, stalks,

An ethanol-powered snowplow in Hennepin County, Minnesota. U.S. Department of Energy.

and cobs) into sugars that can then be converted into ethanol. Historically, the biggest cost component of this technology was the creation of enzymes. Earlier [in 2005], though, in combination with the National Renewable Energy Laboratory, Novozymes announced a 30-fold reduction in the cost of enzyme production in laboratory trials. Expected benefits from this process include low energy requirements, high efficiency, and mild process conditions. A pilot plant exists in Ontario and another is planned in Hawaii. The first commercial-scale enzymatic reduction hydrolysis plant is scheduled to be built and operational by Iogen within two years, producing ethanol at a targeted cost of $1.30 per gallon.

No matter which of these conversion technologies ultimately wins, it is clear that cost-effective and efficient ethanol production from cellulose is on the horizon—which is good news for the United States, where mobility consumes seven of every ten barrels of oil we use. Our voracious appetite for that oil comes at a cost—we have to buy it, we have to deal with the pollution that comes from using it, and, because 12 percent of our oil comes from the Middle East, we have to defend it. Because mobility consumes 70 percent of the oil we use, mostly by burning gasoline, it's the first place to look for a solution.

Ethanol's Payoffs

Our recent publication *Winning the Oil Endgame* shows that the critical first step to reducing our oil consumption is tripled automobile efficiency—which can improve safety, maintain or improve performance and comfort, and repay its extra cost (if any) within two years at today's U.S. gasoline prices. But there's no reason to stop there. Using biofuels instead of gasoline to power our cars has the potential to displace 3.7 million barrels per day of crude oil—that's a fifth of our forecasted consumption in 2025, after more efficient use. In fact, an 85/15 percent blend of ethanol/gasoline in the tank of RMI's designed 66-mpg SUV would result in the vehicle getting ~320 [miles] per gallon of fossil fuel burned (because the majority of fuel burned is ethanol).

Clearly, focusing on the nexus of the agriculture and energy value chains will create huge opportunities for business and huge wins for our country. The critics simply have it wrong.

Plug-in Gasoline-Electric Cars Are Efficient

J. William Moore

J. William Moore is the editor of EV World, *an online journal promoting hybrid vehicles.*

"We think the time has come when car drivers can finally start to have an impact on the kind of cars that are produced," Felix Kramer, the founder of the California Cars Initiative, or CalCars, told me recently. Formed [in 2002] by a group of volunteers from the San Francisco Bay and Southern California areas, the goal of the initiative is to encourage the development of plug-in hybrid-electric cars.

Unlike today's hybrids, which don't require recharge from the electric power grid, plug-in hybrids could be plugged in, an option usually not seen as an advantage, until you start to consider the potential operating cost-savings to consumers, as well as improvements to the local environment.

The batteries would be recharged for essentially pennies to the mile.

Kramer and his group of volunteers, who include engineers and EV [electric vehicle] enthusiasts, set out to raise awareness and funds to finance the development of this cross between a pure battery electric car and a gasoline-electric hybrid, a daunting task in the current economic environment.

But with the introduction of the 2004 model Toyota Prius, Kramer and colleagues think they may have discovered a shortcut to their objective. It's a switch that is on the dash of all new Priuses sold in Japan and Europe, but oddly, not in North

America. It's that missing switch that may be the key to creating the first commercially-available plug-in hybrid, what Cal-Cars considers the "next generation" of hybrid vehicles.

Getting Away from Gasoline

But first a little background. While Honda and Toyota make a point of telling potential buyers they don't have to plug in their gasoline-electric hybrid cars at night to recharge the batteries—their cars' batteries self-recharge while driving—the whole point of grid-connected hybrids is that they do have to be recharged.

The point is to shift the energy inputs from gasoline, 60 percent of which is now imported into the USA, to electric power stored in a larger battery bank on the car. The batteries would be recharged for essentially pennies to the mile from the local power grid using common 110-volt household current, or even from the homeowner's wind generator or solar electric panels. The energy to run the car would come from indigenous, even renewable sources rather than increasingly costly imported petroleum.

It's what Kramer calls "the best of both worlds."

Instead of going to the gasoline station once a week, [hybrid owners] might be able to drive a month or more before having to refuel.

Since most commuters drive no more than 25 miles a day, a plug-in hybrid could have a battery pack sized just large enough to let the driver operate most of the time in zero emission mode like a battery-only EV and then automatically shift to the gasoline-engine when the battery is depleted. The theory is that a smaller battery pack would cost less money.

As Kramer pointed out, the technology exists today and prototypes have already been built. He believes that the only thing left to do is fine-tune the system.

"In addition, there is no new infrastructure needed," he remarked, in obvious reference to the massive investment amounting to hundreds of billions of dollars that will be needed to build a hydrogen refueling system for fuel-cell cars.

From the average consumer's perspective, a 20-miles range grid-hybrid, would mean that instead of going to the gasoline station once a week, they might be able to drive a month or more before having to refuel, Kramer conjectured. While the watts per mile energy consumption of a grid-hybrid has yet to be firmly established, we do know that battery electric vehicles like the Toyota RAV4 EV can be operated at less than 2 cents per mile (275 Watts/mile x 6 cents/kilowatt hr) compared to more than 8 cents a mile on $1.89/gal gasoline. Nighttime, off-peak electric rates would mean even lower operational costs. The only real drawback might be the nightly requirement to plug in the car, a task most battery electric car owners easily adapted to, often commenting how much they liked getting up in the morning with a full tank of "fuel."

According to Kramer, an EPRI [Electric Power Research Institute] study indicated that over the life-time of the car, the total cost of the car would be less than a comparable conventional gasoline vehicle.

"But of course, people don't think that way. The initial cost of the vehicle will be higher," a conclusion based on the fact that advanced batteries like NiMH and Lithium Ion/Polymer are still very expensive, though the cost continues to come down. He anticipates—maybe "hopes" is a better word—that by the time the next generation hybrids become available, lithium batteries will be affordable enough to integrate into the car.

But in a way, this is still the classic chicken-n-egg conundrum; you need light-weight, low-cost, high-power batteries to make grid-hybrids, or PHEVs [plug-in hybrid electric vehicles], feasible and affordable, but you won't see carmakers building them until the batteries come down in price and can offer 150,000 miles or more of operation life.

'Plug-in hybrids are the best transition technology we have and they can start saving energy now.'

Hydrogen Versus Batteries

While the hydrogen bandwagon has been making lots of noise of late, attracting many proponents, as well as critics, Kramer thinks that when we compare the two storage systems, he believes that batteries make more sense than hydrogen, though he agrees that grid-hybrids are still only a transitional technology.

"As I see it, it's always easier to move and to store electrons than it is molecules. So the hydrogen highway is planned to get ready for something that may never happen," he told *EV World*. He's willing to concede that we may see hydrogen fuel-cell vehicles someday, but he wants to see those vehicles also offer a grid-to-vehicle energy architecture where the fuel cell works more as a range-extender, thus reducing the size of the stack and the amount of hydrogen the vehicle has to carry, both ways to reduce the cost of production.

Kramer also expressed a commonly heard concern among electric vehicle advocates and environmentalists, that allowing carmakers to pursue the hydrogen fuel-cell vehicle path, means that little or nothing will be done about reducing emissions and oil imports today, or in the next ten to fifteen years.

"Plug-in hybrids are the best transition technology we have and they can start saving energy now."

Moving Beyond Stealth Mode

What Kramer and other new Toyota Prius owners have discovered is that the car spends a lot of time, especially when creeping along in a traffic jam, in what they have come to call

"Stealth Mode." This is when the car operates only on electric power with its IC [internal combustion] engine turned off, operating much like a battery electric car. And while the battery pack is too small to offer any acceptable speed or range, the Japanese and European versions of the car have a switch on the dash that allows the driver to run the car in electric mode only for short distances up to one or two kilometers at less than 42 mph.

So, some enterprising Prius owners speculated, what would happen if we gave the car a few more batteries?

First, American owners had to find a way to add the missing switch that Toyota unaccountably left off the US version. Since Toyota has failed to reply to my emails and telephone calls, I can't give readers a reason why the switch was not put in US-bound vehicles.

That hasn't stopped a handful of hackers who actually figured out how to tap Toyota's complex computer control system.

"There are a couple of dozen American cars now [that] have added the "EV Only" button," Kramer said, adding that complete instructions on how to do it can be found on the CalCars.org web site, as well as an archive of the online technical dialog.

"That got people thinking. As soon as they got the button going, they started saying 'Wouldn't it be great if we had a longer stealth mode, if we could go longer than a kilometer or two?'" That led to the inevitable conclusion that they needed more batteries.

"The same person [Wayne Brown] who figured out how to reverse-engineer the button has already added additional batteries to his Prius," Kramer explained. The result is a car that gets 10–20 mpg better fuel economy, he said.

The final step in turning the Prius into a grid-connected hybrid is finding a way to recharge the batteries, and according to Kramer, a number of people are at work on the problem, all, it must be noted, without the support or blessing of Toyota Motor Company. In fact, anyone undertaking the installation of the button, much less more batteries, risks voiding their warranty.

Once the final step—and that appears to be the most daunting and risky one of all—has been completed, what you'd have, in Kramer's lexicon is a "neighborhood plug-in hybrid vehicle," a gasoline-electric hybrid with a bit more range than the Japanese/Euro model Priuses with the EV-only button.

"Hypothetically, you'd have a five to fifteen mile range in this vehicle." He sees this as a way to not only let owners run local errands in electric-only mode but, more importantly, get people excited about the concept of plug-it-in hybrids.

Battling Slogans and Market Confusion

Kramer acknowledges that the general public is confused about what a hybrid-electric vehicle is and how it works; most assume, wrongly, that you have to plug it in, which leads Toyota and Honda and now Ford to emphasize the fact that their cars don't need to be recharged. They recharge themselves while you drive.

But plug-in advocates like Kramer and Dr. Andy Frank at UC [University of California] Davis see plugging hybrids in as an advantage, so Kramer's slogan is "You get to plug it in."

What the California Cars Initiative is planning to do is raise enough money to engineer a prototype conversion of a Prius to show that it is feasible. After that, they hope to convert a dozen or so other cars for "well-heeled" owners who are willing to risk their cars, or at the very least void their warranties.

Kramer agreed that given Toyota's prescient engineering culture, that the company probably is already looking at the plug-in hybrid concept, if it hasn't already built a secret prototype or two. He hopes that CalCars' efforts demonstrate to Toyota that there is, in fact, a market for these cars, at least in California, where incomes and grid power mix appear to make this a viable pathway environmentally and economically.

But is there really a market?

Kramer is convinced there is, based on the level of response and enthusiasm he sees for what he calls the Prius+ concept. In addition, he noted that J.D. Powers and Associates reports that 35% of car buyers are interested in hybrid cars and 85% of hybrid car owners would pay more for their cars. To CalCars this represents an opportunity to sell the plug-in concept as a "feature" just like the Prius' GPS navigation system or its self-parking option. "People will pay more for features, some of which have no economic benefit, like leather seats or sun roofs," he said. "So we are pitching this as the best car around, the next generation hybrid."

Hydrogen Will Not Become a Viable Fuel for Many Years

Joseph J. Romm

Joseph J. Romm was acting assistant secretary of energy for energy efficiency and renewable energy during the Clinton administration and is currently the executive director of the Center for Energy and Climate Solutions in Arlington, Virginia.

A whopping two-thirds of U.S. oil consumption is in the transportation sector, the only sector of the U.S. economy wholly reliant on oil. The energy price shocks of the 1970s helped spur growth in use of natural gas for home heating and drove the electric utility sector and the industrial sector to reduce their dependence on petroleum. But roughly 97 percent of all energy consumed by our cars, sport utility vehicles, vans, trucks, and airplanes is still petroleum-based.

The Attraction of Hydrogen

Not surprisingly, a high priority of R&D [research and development] funding by the United States—and by any country, state, or company that takes the long view—is to develop both more fuel-efficient vehicles and alternative fuels. Only a limited number of fuels are plausible alternatives for gasoline, and one enormous benefit of hydrogen over others is that it can be generated by a variety of different sources, thus potentially minimizing dependence on any one. Most important, hydrogen can be generated from renewable sources of energy such as wind power, raising the ultimate prospect of an inexhaustible, clean, domestic source of transportation fuel. Also, since fuel cells are more efficient than gasoline internal combustion engines, hydrogen fuel cell vehicles are, potentially, a double winner in the race to replace oil.

Hydrogen fuel cell vehicles would seem to be the perfect answer to our burgeoning and alarming dependence on imported oil. For some, like Peter Schwartz, chair of the Global Business Network, they are almost the deus ex machina—the quick, pure technological fix—that will avoid the need for difficult policy choices, such as federal mandates for increased vehicle efficiency. That is overoptimistic hype, as we will see.

The pollution generated by internal combustion engine automobiles is another key reason why so many people are drawn to hydrogen fuel cell vehicles. The transportation sector remains one of the largest sources of urban air pollution, especially the oxides of nitrogen that are a precursor to ozone smog and the particulates that do so much damage to our hearts and lungs. Vehicle emissions of such pollutants, however, have been declining steadily, and, by 2010, federal and state standards will have made new U.S. cars exceedingly clean.

If the hydrogen does not come from renewable sources, then it is simply not worth doing.

The Global Warming Threat

Yet, even as new internal combustion engine vehicles dramatically cut the emissions of noxious urban air pollutants by automobiles, their contribution to global warming has begun to rise. In the 1990s, the transportation sector saw the fastest growth in carbon dioxide (CO_2) emissions of any major sector of the U.S. economy. And *the transportation sector is projected to generate nearly half of the 40 percent rise in U.S. CO_2 emissions forecast for 2025.*

When the United States takes serious action on global warming, the transportation sector will need to be a top priority. The two most straightforward ways to reduce vehicle CO_2 emissions are, first, by increasing the fuel efficiency of the vehicles themselves and, second, by using a fuel that has lower net emissions than gasoline. Again, the attractiveness of hydrogen fuel cell vehicles is that they afford the possibility of pursuing both strategies at the same time: Fuel cells are more efficient than traditional internal combustion engines, and hydrogen, when produced from renewable energy sources, would create no net greenhouse gas emissions.

The possibility that hydrogen and fuel cells could play a key role in combating pollution, particularly global warming, is, I believe, the strongest argument for expanded efforts in research and development. John Heywood, director of the Sloan Automotive Laboratory at the Massachusetts Institute of Technology, argues, "If the hydrogen does not come from renewable sources, then it is simply not worth doing, environmentally or economically."

The idea that hydrogen could be generated without releasing any pollution is not a new one. In 1923, John Haldane, who later became one of the century's most famous geneticists, gave a lecture predicting that Britain would ultimately derive its energy from "rows of metallic windmills" generating electricity for the country and, when there was excess wind, producing hydrogen. "Among its more obvious advantages will be the fact that . . . no smoke or ash will be produced."

Until recently, most greenhouse-gas-free sources for hydrogen have been far too expensive to be practical.

Cleaning Up Hydrogen

The problem with the vision of a pure hydrogen economy has been that, until recently, most greenhouse-gas-free sources for hydrogen have been far too expensive to be practical. Haldane himself was imagining a future "four hundred years hence." Even today, nuclear, wind, and solar electric power would produce hydrogen that is far more expensive than hydrogen from fossil fuels. But for more than two decades, renewable energy, especially wind and solar energy, has been declining in price sharply. That has created a renewed interest in renewable hydrogen, although it will still be two or more decades before this is a competitive way to generate hydrogen.

There is another, more unexpected possible source of greenhouse-gas-free hydrogen: fossil fuels. In the mid-1990s, Princeton University professor Bob Williams (and others) produced detailed reports arguing that fossil fuels could be both a cost-effective and an environmentally benign source of hydrogen *if* the CO_2 released during the production process could be captured and stored in underground geologic formations so that it would not be released into the atmosphere and thereby accelerate global warming. His briefings to DOE [Department of Energy] officials and others in government were a major reason why the department launched a major effort to explore this possibility. Today, carbon capture and storage is the subject of considerable research as well as demonstration projects around the globe and is widely seen as a potentially critical strategy for addressing global warming in the longer term.

A hydrogen economy would require dramatic changes in our transportation system.

With ongoing advances in transportation fuel cells and pollution-free hydrogen production, hydrogen vehicles would seem to be the perfect answer to global warming. Yet . . . *hydrogen vehicles are unlikely to make a significant dent in U.S. greenhouse gas emissions in the first half of this century*, especially if U.S. energy policy is not significantly changed. Still, hydrogen-fueled *stationary* power plants could be critical in reducing greenhouse gas emissions much sooner. Further, hydrogen may well be the essential vehicle fuel in the second half of this century if we are to achieve the very deep reductions in CO_2 emissions that will almost certainly be needed then or if we are past the peak of oil production.

We are not used to thinking or planning in such giant, multi-decade time steps. But then again, we have never faced such a giant problem as global warming.

Still Out of Reach

The term "hydrogen economy" describes a time when a substantial fraction of our energy is delivered by hydrogen made from sources of energy that have no net emissions of greenhouse gases. These would include renewable sources of energy, such as wind power and biomass (e.g., plant matter), but it could also include the scenario of converting fossil fuels into hydrogen and CO_2 and then permanently storing the carbon. It could also include generating hydrogen from nuclear power, should that prove practical.

We are unlikely to know whether a hydrogen economy is practical and economically feasible for at least one decade and possibly two or even more. A hydrogen economy would require dramatic changes in our transportation system because, at room temperature and pressure, hydrogen takes up three thousand times more space than gasoline containing an equivalent amount of energy. We will need tens of thousands of hydrogen fueling stations, and, unless hydrogen is generated on-site at those stations, we will also need a massive infrastructure for delivering that hydrogen from wherever it is generated.

Substantial technological and cost breakthroughs will be needed in many areas, not the least of which is fuel cells for vehicles. In 2003, fuel cell vehicles cost $1 million each or more. Were we to build a hydrogen infrastructure for fueling vehicles, the total delivered cost of hydrogen generated from fossil fuel sources would likely be at least triple the cost of gasoline for the foreseeable future. Hydrogen generated from renewable energy sources would be considerably more expensive. Hydrogen storage is currently expensive, inefficient, and subject to onerous codes and standards. The DOE does not foresee making a decision about commercializing fuel cell vehicles until 2015. One detailed 2003 analysis of a hydrogen economy by two leading European fuel cell experts concluded, "The 'pure-hydrogen-only-solution' may never become reality."

And if the imposing technical and cost problems can be substantially solved, we will still have an imposing chicken-and-egg problem: Who will spend hundreds of billions of dollars on a wholly new nationwide infrastructure to provide ready access to hydrogen for consumers with fuel cell vehicles until millions of hydrogen vehicles are on the road? Yet who will manufacture and market such vehicles—and who will buy them—until the infrastructure is in place to fuel those vehicles? A 2002 analysis by Argonne National Laboratory found that "with current technologies, the hydrogen delivery infrastructure to serve 40% of the light duty fleet is likely to cost over $500 billion." I fervently hope to see an economically, environmentally, and politically plausible scenario for bridging this classic catch-22 chasm; it does not yet exist.

Vegetable Oil Should Not Replace Conventional Diesel Fuel

Alexis Ziegler

Alexis Ziegler is a writer and activist working on environment, transportation, and media issues.

B iodiesel is the fastest-growing alternative fuel in the US. For its proponents, biodiesel promises to deliver us into an age of clean and renewable fuel. Yet if present trends continue, biodiesel is more likely to escalate human misery around the world for years to come.

Biodiesel's proponents claim that they are recycling discarded cooking oil. But is that oil really waste? In my hometown of Charlottesville, Virginia, used oil is collected by one of the four largest rendering companies in the US—Valley Proteins, which reprocesses dead animals, inedible slaughterhouse remains and used cooking oil into a wide variety of products. From a financial report, we learn that "Valley Proteins turns the raw materials it collects into commodity goods, which are sold to over 170 customers. . . . The company's finished products are quoted on established commodity markets or priced relative to substitute commodities. . . ." About 80 percent of the fats from rendering are used in livestock feed. The rest are reprocessed into other products, including pet foods, chemicals and lubricants.

Note the phrase, "products are . . . priced relative to substitute commodities." Used cooking oil is not a discarded product—it is reprocessed and put on the market to vie with "substitute commodities." Any of the many companies using

Alexis Ziegler, "Biodiesel; Salvation or Disaster?," *Earth First! Journal*, vol. 25, May-June 2005, p. 40. Copyright © 2005 Daily Planet Publishing. Reproduced by permission.

products from Valley Proteins is likely to purchase the cheapest adequate product, regardless of its source. If the buyers should run short of used vegetable oil, they would simply turn to products made from virgin oil instead.

Biodiesel potentially involves taking human food, like soy, corn, and other oil-producing plants, and feeding it to automobiles.

Food or Fuel?

If biodiesel consumption were to remain within the supply of used vegetable oil, that would all be fine. The problem is that the consumption of fossil diesel radically exceeds the supply of used oil. Americans use nearly a billion gallons of petroleum a day; the entire output of all of the rendering companies in the US is a billion and a half gallons per year. If the entire annual output of used vegetable oil were diverted into the fossil fuel market, it would last us 36 hours. And that simply begs the question of where industry would turn to for all that cattle feed.

Is biodiesel renewable? Any resource is renewable only if it is extracted at a rate no greater than it is replenished. Overcutting a forest or overfishing a fishery renders a renewable resource non-renewable. Given that biodiesel potentially involves taking human food, like soy, corn and other oil-producing plants, and feeding it to automobiles, the renewability issue is paramount.

If we are going to feed human food to cars, we should take stock of the status of the global food production system. In 2004, global grain stocks were reduced to their lowest point in 30 years. Do you know when the world fish catch peaked? In the early 1980s. Irrigated farmland produces a lion's share of human food, but the global supply of irrigated farmland per capita has shrunk considerably. Even though the US has the most productive agricultural system in the world, it now teeters on the brink of agricultural debtorship. Beginning in the 1990s, the United States has imported more food than it has exported in some years.

Given that the amount of farmland per person, irrigated and not, has substantially decreased, how is it that we continue to feed growing populations? Because we have been replacing soil with oil. Worldwide, the amount of energy we invest in each calorie of food has climbed steadily with increased use of chemical fertilizers, pesticides and herbicides. According to David Pimentel, a researcher at Cornell University, American agriculture now invests three calories of fossil fuel for each calorie it produces. That is long before anyone considers putting those food calories into a gas tank.

Market Forces

If biodiesel is ecologically expensive, then won't the market correct the problem by keeping biodiesel financially expensive? Maybe, but for biodiesel's extra edge—guilt relief. There are a lot of progressive Americans who want to help the environment, but whose lifestyle is as car dependent as anyone else's. In Fall 2004, Congress passed an excise tax relief to encourage the use of biodiesel. The horse is out of the gate.

If Americans are convinced that biodiesel is a "green" fuel, and we drive up the consumption of vegetable oil, we simply shift the weight of demand onto the virgin vegetable oil market. That isn't just a theory. In my home state of Virginia, the Soybean Association has been offering a cash rebate for first-time biodiesel purchases of up to $500. The only motivation for such action is to bolster the price of virgin oil. This isn't about used fryer oil any longer.

Biodiesel is a powerful movement that is rapidly gaining force. As cars with their savage buying power are put into market competition with the hundreds of millions of humans already trying to live on a dollar a day, the latter will lose the tug of war. The global poor, for whom vegetable oil is already a scarce item, will do without.

All of this begs the question: If not biodiesel, then what? We have to have some source of energy, for transportation and otherwise. The issue is whether you work on the problem from the demand side or the supply side.

Supply and Demand

If you take any modern energy system and try to address it from the supply side, you will fail. Already, there is a movement to use biofuels to generate the nation's electricity. That means that massive tree-chipping operations have started descending on our national forests, converting lush, green ecosystems into moonscape and chips. The chips are then burned instead of coal to generate electricity, thus keeping the tumble [clothes] driers of America in operation. If you try to meet US energy demands from the supply side, you are simply going to throw unsustainable weight onto already overstressed biological systems.

Neither can we deal with transportation fuel by attacking the problem from the supply side. According to Pimentel, biofuels such as ethanol represent a net energy loss. Even if we disregard the energy used to distill ethanol, about 11 acres of corn must be used to fuel one car for one year—but the global supply of grain-land per person was .57 acres (notice the decimal) in 1950, and is projected to be .17 acres in 2050. Biodiesel represents similar ecological absurdities, yet both biodiesel and ethanol have Congressional support. How we do cherish the myth of technology.

If you try to get your energy from any "alternative" source, the same supply-side principle applies. If you tried to supply the average American household with photovoltaic panels, it would cost hundreds of thousands of dollars. Not only is that financially unfeasible, but the panels themselves represent a huge environmental cost. The only feasible way to supply a household with alternative energy is to first dramatically reduce the energy consumption of that household.

Biofuels perpetuate the myth that our [energy intensive] lifestyle can continue, if only we find the right fuel.

Alternatives to Fuel

Why are we trying to solve our ecological problems with all the wrong answers? Because the right answers challenge our lifestyle. It is absolutely impossible to support the American lifestyle in a sustainable fashion with any energy source. Biofuels are not merely a neutral bystander; they are enormously destructive. Supply-side biofuels perpetuate the myth that our lifestyle can continue, if only we find the right fuel—biodiesel, ethanol, hydrogen, etc. "President" Bush supports hydrogen; Congress supports biodiesel and ethanol. Think about it.

Single-family housing, as well as individual automobiles, are simply unsustainable, regardless of our energy source. So what then are the solutions? Live close enough to where you work and play so that you don't have to drive. Refuse to own a car. Live cooperatively. For mainstream liberals, that may sound absurd. But that is precisely why the entire discussion about biofuels is misguided, because real solutions demand a more radical perspective. Real answers are social and ecological, not technological. Turning the beast of industrialism with its voracious appetite away from fossil fuel and into our forests and fields is not an answer.

Ethanol Has Hidden Costs

Ben Lieberman

Ben Lieberman is senior policy analyst in the Thomas A. Roe Institute for Economic Policy Studies at the Heritage Foundation, a conservative Washington, D.C., think tank.

Editor's note: The bill discussed in this viewpoint did not pass, but a similar one was signed into law in August 2005. Included was a renewable fuels standard that will increase ethanol production to 7.5 billion gallons per year by 2012.

Included in the pending [in April 2005] energy bill are provisions requiring the use of ethanol in the gasoline supply. This proposed ethanol mandate would raise the cost of gasoline, running against the original purpose of the energy bill—to make energy more affordable. For that reason, the mandate should have no place in the energy bill.

Ethanol, a corn-derived motor fuel additive, has long benefited from favorable tax treatment and federal regulations encouraging its use. But its sales have not grown quickly enough to satisfy the ethanol industry or its allies in Congress.

A 5 billion gallon mandate was included in an earlier version of the energy bill that was narrowly defeated, on other grounds, in 2003. The House reintroduced its energy bill, with the 5 billion gallon mandate, while the Senate has two proposals in the works—for 6 billion and 8 billion gallons. Any of these targets could become part of the final version of the bill. The President has already signaled his support for increased ethanol use, citing both its domestic origin and benefits to the agricultural sector.

Ben Lieberman, "Keep Ethanol Out of the Energy Bill," The Heritage Foundation Web-Memo #713, April 8, 2005. The Heritage Foundation. Reproduced by permission.

While an ethanol mandate would benefit Midwestern corn farmers and ethanol producers, it would make gasoline more expensive for everyone. Indeed, the only reason ethanol needs federal help is that it is too expensive to compete on its own. Whether 5 billion, 6 billion, or 8 billion gallons, an ethanol mandate would mean significant cost increases for the driving public.

In Washington, the ethanol lobby has become a powerful special interest.

Regulations and Ethanol

In 1978, President [Jimmy] Carter signed the Energy Tax Act, which encouraged the use of fuel ethanol by partially exempting it from the federal gasoline tax. Though intended only to help the fledgling ethanol industry establish itself, this tax break has persisted and was recently renewed through 2010. The current tax credit is 52 cents for each gallon of pure ethanol. Thus, a blend of 10 percent ethanol and 90 percent gasoline receives a 5.2-cent reduction from the 18.4 cent per gallon federal gas tax. This tax credit helps offset ethanol's higher cost relative to gasoline.

Other federal laws and regulations also encourage the use of ethanol. Since 1996, the Clean Air Act has required many of the nation's largest metropolitan areas to use reformulated gasoline (RFG). Originally intended to reduce summer smog, RFG now comprises one-third of the nation's fuel supply. RFG must contain 2 percent oxygen content by weight. This necessitates the addition of oxygenates, either methyl tertiary butyl ether (MTBE) or ethanol.

MTBE is cheaper than ethanol and was initially more popular. But concerns about MTBE contamination of water supplies have led several states to ban its use. Last year [2004], for example, both New York and California put bans in place, forcing a switch to ethanol in those states. Thus, ethanol use has increased in recent years, from less than 2 billion gallons in 2001 to a record 3.5 billion gallons in 2004.

In addition to the Clean Air Act, tax credits for small ethanol producers and assistance and price supports for corn farmers also serve to promote ethanol. These provisions were enacted through the efforts of Midwestern legislators. Most ethanol production facilities—as well as the corn grown to supply them—are located in Iowa, Illinois, Nebraska, Minnesota, Missouri, Kansas, Indiana, and other Midwestern states. In Washington, the ethanol lobby has become a powerful special interest, benefiting from both strong bipartisan support among the region's legislators and only sporadic opposition from those representing the rest of the country.

Doubts over the environmental benefits of using oxygenates in RFG led to provisions in previous versions of the energy bill to eliminate the oxygenate requirement. But this would jeopardize ethanol sales. For this reason, the ethanol lobby insists on replacing the requirement with a "renewable fuels" standard, which would effectively mandate 5 billion gallons or more of annual use by 2012. No surprise, ethanol is the primary renewable fuel that would benefit from the standard, with other agriculturally derived fuels making up only a small percentage of the total. Versions of the energy bill containing this provision have repeatedly passed the House but stalled in the Senate, on other grounds. . . .

The Impact of an Ethanol Mandate

There is little doubt that federal ethanol policy has increased the cost of gasoline. Much of that cost is hidden from consumers and not seen at the pump due to the preferential tax treatment that masks the true cost of ethanol. An ethanol mandate would increase this cost further.

A 2002 Energy Information Administration study of the energy bill's impact put the cost of the 5 billion gallon ethanol mandate at no more than one cent per gallon, but there is good reason to believe that the cost could be higher. Raising ethanol production to 6 or 8 billion gallons would increase costs disproportionately: The higher the level of production, the more pressure on corn prices, and the harder it is for ethanol producers to meet demand. Larger ethanol targets also mean that more of it will have to be used outside of the Midwest. Since ethanol cannot be distributed through pipelines, the cost of transporting it long distances will be high.

Overall, an ethanol mandate could end up adding several cents to the price of a gallon of gasoline—a burden that American motorists hardly need.

The ethanol mandate is an anti-consumer provision. It benefits special interests at the expense of the driving public. As such, it has no place in an energy bill that seeks to make energy more affordable for the American people.

Gasoline-Electric Cars Do Not Reduce Fuel Use

David Leonhardt

David Leonhardt is a business and economics columnist for the New York Times.

Some of my favorite people drive a Prius. They bought the car, obviously, because they were worried about the planet. But the fringe benefits are pretty nice, too.

Prius drivers can use a carpool lane in some places even when no one else is in the car. No matter where they're driving, they coast down the road in a whisper-quiet hum unlike anything else. Best of all, even if no one likes admitting it, they get to enjoy the cool-kid cachet that comes with being an early adopter of a fad. No other vehicle has had a recurring role on the TV show "Curb Your Enthusiasm."

Now President [George W.] Bush has taken the hybrid craze to a whole new level. To cure our addiction to oil, he said [in his 2006 State of the Union address], we must invest in hybrid cars, hydrogen cars, even cars that run on wood chips and grass. Energy technology is having its big moment.

Too bad the benefits of our new cult car have been so exaggerated.

Hybrids have the most overblown mileage ratings in the auto industry.

Questionable Mileage

Let's start with the obvious advantage of hybrids. When you drive one, you burn less gas than you would in a regular car. A typical driver of a Prius will use about 250 fewer gallons of gasoline each year than somebody would in a Toyota Corolla, which gets 29 miles a gallon. That's doing everyone else a favor because gas use has other costs—like global warming and American troops stationed overseas—that nobody fully pays at the pump.

But the favor is not nearly as big as hybrid owners imagine, for two reasons. First, hybrids have the most overblown mileage ratings in the auto industry. In the government's road tests, which are conducted in a world without much traffic or any air-conditioning, the Prius gets 55 miles to the gallon. *Consumer Reports* says the car really goes 44 miles on a gallon of gas. When I used one . . . —and there is no denying that it's a great car to drive—I got 45 in Manhattan and on local highways.

This is just the beginning of the story. The more time you spend looking at the economics of the hybrids, the less comfortable you get.

The most important reason is a government policy that, amazingly enough, seems almost intended to undercut the benefits of efficient cars. In 1978, Congress set a minimum corporate average fuel economy, known as CAFE, for all carmakers. Today, the minimum average for cars is 27.5 miles a gallon. (For S.U.V.'s and other light trucks, it is 21.6.)

Instead of simply saving gas when you buy a hybrid, you're giving somebody else the right to use it.

Fuel Use Is Not Reduced

You can guess what this means for hybrids. Each one becomes a free pass for its manufacturer to sell a few extra gas guzzlers. For now, this is less true for Toyota's cars, because they're above the mileage requirement. But Toyota's trucks and the American automakers are right near the limits. So every Toyota Highlander hybrid S.U.V. begets a hulking Lexus S.U.V., and every Ford Escape—the hybrid S.U.V. that Kermit the Frog hawked during Super Bowl [XL]—makes room for a Lincoln Navigator, which gets all of 12 miles a gallon. Instead of simply saving gas when you buy a hybrid, you're giving somebody else the right to use it.

The hybrid, then, is just about the perfect example of what's wrong with our energy policy. It's a Band-Aid that does a lot less to help the earth than we like to tell ourselves. When Vice President Dick Cheney dismissed conservation as "a sign of personal virtue" a few years back, a lot of environmentalists were disgusted. But that, sadly, is what a lot of well-meaning hybrid owners are driving: an expensive symbol that they're worried about our planet, rather than a true solution.

You can consider yourself a conservationist and still see the logic in this. As Jon Coifman, the media director of the Natural Resources Defense Council, says, "We're not going to kick our oil addiction with good will and personal virtue. You do need market signals, and you do need rules. And you need virtue. You need it all."

The simplest idea in economics, I think, is that people respond to the incentives they are given. It's why market economies have done so well. So if we have decided that we need to use less oil for our own good—which seems to be the case—we need big incentives to change our behavior.

Other Paths to Energy Savings

A substantial gas tax would be the simplest, with other taxes being cut to keep down the overall burden. Car buyers could drive whatever they wanted, as long as they were paying the full cost of their gas, and automakers would respond with creative products. If we're not capable of having a serious discussion about new taxes, the second-best option would be lavish incentives for companies to sell a fuel-efficient fleet.

Jonathan Skinner, an economist at Dartmouth [College], has a nice way of thinking about this. Forget about the 250 gallons of gas that a Prius saves relative to a Corolla. An S.U.V. that gets 16 miles a gallon, like the Cadillac SRX, uses almost 600 fewer gallons annually than an 11-mile-a-gallon Hummer H2, because small differences add up when gas is being burned so quickly. It's the person deciding between those two vehicles who needs some extra incentives.

Instead, the government is giving $3,000 tax credits to hybrid buyers and opening carpool lanes to them. As a result, some people are buying cars they don't need. So get this: Americans are now replacing perfectly good cars, like the Corolla, in the name of conservation.

There is one sign of improvement. The Environmental Protection Agency [E.P.A.] has announced that it is fixing its fuel-economy ratings. The stickers that appear on the windows of new cars will soon show more realistic mileage numbers.

Unfortunately, the E.P.A. is in charge of only the stickers. The Department of Transportation makes the fuel-economy rules—the ones that actually matter—and it's not planning any changes. It will proceed with the fiction that the Prius gets 55 miles to the gallon. This is our energy policy.

Organizations to Contact

Cato Institute
1000 Massachusetts Ave. NW, Washington, DC   20001-5403
(202) 842-0200 • fax: (202) 842-3490
e-mail: cato@cato.org
Web site: www.cato.org

The Cato Institute is a libertarian public policy research foundation that aims to limit the role of government and protect civil liberties. Publications offered on its Web site include the bimonthly *Cato Policy Report* and the quarterly journal *Regulation*. Both publications frequently contain articles on energy issues.

Competitive Enterprise Institute (CEI)
1001 Connecticut Ave. NW, Suite 1250, Washington, DC
   20036
(202) 331-1010 • fax: (202) 331-0640
e-mail: info@cei.org
Web site: www.cei.org

CEI is a nonprofit public policy organization founded on the principle that free enterprise, limited government, and private incentives, rather than government regulations, are the basis of sound policy, including energy policy. CEI's publications include the newsletter *Monthly Planet* (formerly *CEI Update*), *Enviro Wire*, and the book *The Environmental Source*. All CEI publications periodically feature articles on energy alternatives.

Evangelical Environmental Network (EEN)
10 E. Lancaster Ave., Wynnewood, PA   19096-3495
(202) 554-1955
e-mail: een@creationcare.org
Web site: www.creationcare.org

EEN is a faith-based ministry whose members encourage the Christian community to work together for biblical steward-ship and protection of the earth's environment through cam-paigns such as "What Would Jesus Drive?" The organization's main publication is *Creation Care*, a quarterly magazine.

Foundation for Clean Air Progress (FCAP)

e-mail: info@cleanairprogress.org

Web site: www.cleanairprogress.org

FCAP is a nonprofit organization that believes that the public is unaware of the progress that has been made in reducing air pollution. The foundation represents various sectors of busi-ness and industry in providing information to the public about improving air quality trends. FCAP publishes reports and studies demonstrating that air pollution is on the decline, including "Breathing Easier About Energy—A Healthy Economy and Healthier Air" and "Study on Air Quality Trends, 1970–2015."

Greenpeace U.S.A.

702 H St. NW, Washington, DC   20001

(202) 462-1177 • fax: (202) 462-4507

e-mail: greenpeace@wdc.greenpeace.org

Web site: www.greenpeace.org

Greenpeace opposes nuclear energy and supports renewables. It uses direct-action techniques and strives for media coverage of its actions in an effort to educate the public about environ-mental issues. The organization's publications include the re-ports "Offshore Wind—Implementing a New Power House for Europe" and "Fueling Global Warming."

The Heritage Foundation

214 Massachusetts Ave. NE, Washington, DC   20002-4999

(202) 546-4400 • fax: (202) 546-8328

e-mail: info@heritage.org
Web site: www.heritage.org

The Heritage Foundation is a conservative think tank that supports the principles of free enterprise and limited government in energy issues. Its publications on energy include an extensive list of memos on the foundation's Web site and the report "Econometric and Policy Evaluation of the National Energy Policy."

Office of Energy Efficiency and Renewable Energy (EERE)
Mail Stop EE-1, Washington, DC   20585
(202) 586-9220
e-mail: eeremailbox@ee.doe.gov
Web site: www.eere.energy.gov

The EERE is a project of the U.S. Department of Energy. Its mission is to strengthen America's energy security, environmental quality, and economic vitality by disseminating information on renewable and efficient energy use. EERE publishes *Clean Cities Now*, a newsletter promoting alternative fuel vehicles.

Office of Fossil Energy
U.S. Department of Energy, Washington, DC   20585
(202) 586-6503 • fax: (212) 586-5146
e-mail: fewebmaster@hq.doe.gov
Web site: www.fe.doe.gov

The Office of Fossil Energy is a branch of the U.S. Department of Energy that promotes higher environmental, health, and safety standards in the use of fossil fuels. It publishes *Fossil Energy Techlines*, a monthly online update on energy issues and news.

Pew Center on Global Climate Change
2101 Wilson Blvd., Suite 550, Arlington, VA   22201
(703) 516-4146 • fax: (703) 841-1422
Web site: www.pewclimate.org

The Pew Center is a nonpartisan organization dedicated to educating the public and policy makers about the causes and potential consequences of global climate change and informing them of ways to reduce the emissions of greenhouse gases. Its reports include "Towards a Climate-Friendly Built Environment" and "U.S. Electric Power Sector and Climate Change Mitigation."

Reason Foundation

3415 S. Sepulveda Blvd., Suite. 400
  Los Angeles, CA   90034-6064
(310) 391-2245 • fax: (310) 391-4395
e-mail: feedback@reason.org
Web site: www.reason.org

The Reason Foundation is a libertarian public policy research organization. Its environmental research focuses on issues such as energy, global warming, and air quality. The foundation publishes the monthly magazine *Reason* as well as studies, including "Digging Our Way Out of the ANWR Morass: A Performance-Based Approach to Protecting Habitat and Managing Resources" and "Fueling America: How Hydrogen Cars Affect the Environment."

Renewable Energy Policy Project/Center for Renewable Energy and Sustainable Technology (REPP/CREST)

1612 K St. NW, Suite. 202, Washington, DC   20006
(202) 293-2898 • fax: (202) 298-5357
e-mail: info2@repp.org
Web site: www.repp.org

REPP/CREST's mission is to promote renewable energy technology through research and public education. Recent publications of the organizations include the papers "Geothermal Energy Issue Brief" and "Wind Energy for Electric Power."

Rocky Mountain Institute
1739 Snowmass Creek Rd., Snowmass, CO   81654-9199
(970) 927-3851 • fax: (970) 927-4510
Web site: www.rmi.org

The Rocky Mountain Institute is a nonprofit organization providing research and consulting on issues including energy efficiency and sustainable use of resources. In addition to a newsletter, *RMI Solutions*, the institute publishes books and reports on energy, including *Winning the Oil Endgame* and *Small Is Profitable.*

Union of Concerned Scientists (UCS)
2 Brattle Sq., Cambridge, MA   02238
(617) 547-5552 • fax: (617) 864-9405
e-mail: ucs@ucsusa.org
Web site: www.ucsusa.org

UCS aims to advance responsible public policy in areas where science and technology play important roles. Its programs emphasize safe and renewable energy technologies, transportation reform, arms control, and sustainable agriculture. UCS publications include the twice-yearly magazine *Catalyst*, the quarterly newsletter *Earthwise*, and the report "Greener SUVs."

U.S. Public Interest Research Group (U.S. PIRG)
218 D St. SE, Washington, DC   20003
(202) 546-9707 • fax: (202) 546-2461
e-mail: uspirg@pirg.org
Web site: www.uspirg.org

U.S. PIRG is a grassroots nonprofit group that advocates on behalf of citizen interests and the environment. The national organization and affiliated state chapters work on a wide range of issues, including energy, transportation, and pollution. In addition to its quarterly newsletter *U.S. PIRG Citizen Agenda*, the organization publishes frequent reports, including "Solutions to America's Oil Crisis: A Federal Agenda for Reducing Oil Demand and Protecting Consumers" and "Going Nowhere: The Price Consumers Pay for Stalled Fuel Economy Policies."

World Bank
Environment Department, Washington, DC   20433
(202) 477-1234 • fax: (202) 577-0565
Web site: www.worldbank.org

The World Bank seeks to reduce poverty and improve the standards of living of poor people around the world. It promotes sustainable growth and investments in developing countries through loans, technical assistance, and policy guidance. Many of the bank's projects focus on energy. Publications from the bank's Environment Department include the Discussion Paper Series, which explores a wide variety of issues related to energy sector reform, and the report "The Energy Challenge for Achieving the Millennium Development Goals."

Worldwatch Institute
1776 Massachusetts Ave. NW, Washington, DC   20036-1904
(202) 452-1999 • fax: (202) 296-7365
e-mail: worldwatch@worldwatch.org
Web site: www.worldwatch.org

Worldwatch is a nonprofit public policy research organization dedicated to informing the public and policy makers about emerging global problems and trends and the complex links between the environment and the world economy. Among its many publications are included *Vital Signs*, issued every year, the bimonthly magazine *World Watch*, and the "Renewables 2005: Global Status Report."

Bibliography

Books

Curtis D. Anderson and Judy Anderson	*Electric and Hybrid Cars: A History.* Jefferson, NC: McFarland, 2005.
Harvey Blatt	*America's Environmental Report Card: Are We Making the Grade?* Cambridge, MA: MIT Press, 2005.
Godfrey Boyle	*Renewable Energy: Power for a Sustainable Future.* New York: Oxford University Press, 2004.
Lester Brown	*Rescuing a Planet Under Stress and a Civilization in Trouble.* New York: Norton, 2003.
Rebecca L. Busby	*Hydrogen and Fuel Cells: A Comprehensive Guide.* Tulsa, OK: PennWell Corp., 2005.
Kenneth F. Deffeyes	*Beyond Oil: The View from Hubbert's Peak.* New York: Hill & Wang, 2005.
John M. Deutch	*Making Technology Work: Applications in Energy and the Environment.* New York: Cambridge University Press, 2004.
Lynn Ellen Dokon	*The Alcohol Fuel Handbook.* West Conshohocken, PA: Infinity, 2001.

Ross Gelbspan	*Boiling Point: How Politicians, Big Oil and Coal, Journalists and Activists Are Fueling the Climate Crisis and What We Can Do to Avert Disaster.* New York: Basic Books, 2005.
Paul Gipe	*Wind Power: Renewable Energy for Home, Farm and Business.* White River Junction, VT: Chelsea Green, 2004.
Elizabeth Grossman	*Watershed: The Undamming of America.* Jackson, TN: Counterpoint, 2002.
Scott W. Heaberlin	*A Case for Nuclear Generated Electricity.* Columbus, OH: Battle Press, 2003.
Peter W. Huber and Mark P. Mills	*The Bottomless Well: The Twilight of Fuel, the Virtue of Waste, and Why We Will Never Run Out of Energy.* New York: Basic Books, 2005.
Mark Jaccard	*Sustainable Fossil Fuels: The Unusual Suspect in the Quest for Clean and Enduring Energy.* Cambridge, MA: Cambridge University Press, 2005.
Michael T. Klare	*Blood and Oil: The Dangers and Consequences of America's Growing Dependency on Imported Petroleum.* New York: Metropolitan Books, 2004.
Paul Komor	*Renewable Energy Policy.* Lincoln, NE: iUniverse, 2004.

Greg Pahl   *Biodiesel: Growing a New Energy
                   Economy.* White River Junction, VT:
                   Chelsea Green, 2005.

Doug Pratt   *Got Sun? Go Solar: Get Free Renew-
                   able Energy to Power Your Grid-Tied
                   Home.* Massonville, CO: PixyJack
                   Press, 2005.

Vaclav Smil   *Energy at the Crossroads.* Cambridge,
                   MA: MIT Press, 2005.

Christine   *The Homeowners Guide to Energy
Woodside   Independence: Alternative Power
                   Sources for the Average American.*
                   Guilford, CT: Lyons Press, 2006.

Periodicals

Associated Press   "Research Shows Ethanol Isn't Worth
                   the Money," July 17, 2005.
                   www.msnbc.msn.com/.

Dan Bihn   "Wood Heating for All?" *Solar Today,*
                   November/December 2005.

Maryann Bird   "Power to the People," *Time Europe,*
                   May 1, 2005.

John Carey, Adam   "Alternative Power: A Change Is in
Aston, Justin   the Wind," *Business Week,* July 4,
Hibbard, and   2005.
Ronald Glover

Joel Darmstadter   "Whistling in the Wind? Toward a
                   Realistic Pursuit of Renewable En-
                   ergy," *Brookings Review,* Spring 2002.

Daphne Eviatar — "Africa's Oil Tycoons," *Nation*, April 12, 2004.

Alexandra Goho — "Energy on Ice," *Science News*, June 25, 2005.

Amanda Griscom-Little — "Shooting the Moon," *American Prospect*, October 2005.

Dr. Scott Kohl — "Agriculture's Role in Ensuring U.S. Energy Independence," *Feed and Grain*, August/September 2005.

James Howard Kunstler — "End of the Binge," *American Conservative*, September 12, 2005.

Stefan Lovgren — "Spray-On Solar-Power Cells Are True Breakthrough," *National Geographic News*, January 14, 2005. www.news.nationalgeographic.com/.

Emily Matthews — "Undying Flame: The Continuing Demand for Wood as Fuel," *EarthTrends*, 2005.

Jack Nerad — "Hydrogen Fuel from Ethanol?" *Driving Today*, August 23, 2005.

James M. Pethokoukis — "A New Look at Nukes: Energy Firms Push to Build Reactors as Natural Gas Prices Soar," *U.S. News & World Report*, September 26, 2005.

Virginia Phillips — "Clean Energy Special: Eastern Promise," *New Scientist*, September 3, 2005.

Kara Platoni   "Bug Juice: Could Termite Guts Hold
                    the Key to the World's Energy Prob-
                    lems? Don't Laugh," *East Bay Express*,
                    September 7, 2005. www.eastbayex-
                    press.com.

Alan Reynolds   "Redesigning Trucks in Washington,"
                    Human Events, August 25, 2005.

Paul Roberts   "Got Gas? Oil Isn't the Only Fossil
                    Fuel That's in Crisis," *Slate.com* May
                    11, 2004. www.slate.com.

Arthur Smith   "The Case for Space-Based Solar
                    Power Development," *Space Daily*,
                    August 11, 2003. www.spacedaily.
                    com.

Tim Sramcik   "Fueling Around," *Aftermarket Busi-
                    ness*, November, 2004.

Ronald J.   "The High Costs of Federal Energy
Sutherland   Efficiency: Standards for Residential
                    Appliances," Cato Institute, December
                    23, 2003. www.cato.org.

Jerry Taylor   "Not Cheap, Not Green," *Washington
                    Times*, August 4, 2003.

R. James Woolsey   "Defeating the Oil Weapon," *Com-
                    mentary*, September 2002.

Index